TEENAGE violence

Other Books by Elaine Landau

Child Abuse
  An American Epidemic
  Revised Edition

Different Drummer
  Homosexuality in America

The Homeless

On the Streets
  The Lives of Adolescent Prostitutes

Teenagers Talk about School

Why Are They Starving Themselves?
  Understanding Anorexia Nervosa and Bulimia

ELAINE LANDAU

TEENAGE
violence

JULIAN MESSNER

Copyright © 1990 by Elaine Landau
All rights reserved including the right of
reproduction in whole or in part in any form.
Published by Julian Messner, a division of
Silver Burdett Press, Inc., Simon & Schuster, Inc.
Prentice Hall Bldg., Englewood Cliffs, NJ 07632.

JULIAN MESSNER and colophon are trademarks of
Simon & Schuster, Inc.   Design by Liz Fox
Manufactured in the United States of America.

Lib. ed.   10 9 8 7 6 5 4 3 2 1
Paper ed. 10 9 8 7 6 5 4 3 2 1

Library of Congress Cataloging-in-Publication Data

Landau, Elaine.
    Teenage violence /Elaine Landau
        p.   cm.
    Includes bibliographical references.
    Summary: Discusses specific cases of teenage
violence, including satanic cult activities, racial and
sexual attacks, gang violence, acquaintance rape,
and school violence. Examines why teens exhibit
aggressive behavior and surveys the juvenile justice
system.
    1. Juvenile delinquency—United States—Case
studies—Juvenile literature.   2. Violent crimes—
United States—Case studies—Juvenile literature.
3. Violence in children—Juvenile literature.
[1. Violence.   2. Violent crimes.   3. Juvenile
delinquency.]
I. Title
HV9104.L28   1990
364.3'6'0973—dc20   89-49587
ISBN 0-671-70153-3 ISBN 0-671-70154-1 (pbk) CIP
                                                        AC

Contents

In memory of Yusuf K. Hawkins

1973–1989

TEENAGE

violence

CHAPTER

1

The American Dream

It was supposed to have been the American dream. Yusuf K. Hawkins, a black sixteen-year-old honor student, was about to purchase his first car. He had seen an ad for a used Pontiac in a weekly shopper's guide. Maybe now it was Yusuf's turn to enjoy a piece of the dream—to acquire a possession often considered symbolic of emergence into manhood. To many young men, a car is more than just a mode of transportation; it's often associated with freedom, independence, and adulthood.

Therefore, it's not surprising that the teenager sounded excited when he called to find out more about the vehicle. Hawkins also sounded knowledgeable as he inquired about the car's mileage and engine problems. He asked for directions to Bensonhurst, the predominantly white section of Brooklyn, New York, where the car's owner resided.

The person at the other end of the phone was Nick Hadzinas, a twenty-five-year-old construction worker who had come to America from Salonika, Greece, just over two years earlier. Hadzinas left his homeland to find a better life in America or, as a friend described it, "because he planned on living the American dream."[1]

It was arranged that Hawkins would stop by that evening to inspect the car. But as the night wore on, Hadzinas dozed off on his living room couch while waiting for the young potential buyer, who'd missed the appointment. Hadzinas later told police that when Hawkins didn't arrive, he thought that the young man had changed his mind.

But that's not what happened. Instead, Yusuf Hawkins met a devastating fate that night. Following Hadzinas's directions, he took the subway train to Bensonhurst. He was accompanied by three of his friends who he hoped would help him reach a decision about the car. The boys arrived in Bensonhurst, but they never made it to Hadzinas's residence.

According to New York City prosecutors, the four young men were jumped by a gang of about ten angry white youths. The whites, armed with baseball bats and other blunt instruments, chased and cornered the black sixteen-year-old and his friends. Someone in the mob shouted, "Let's club the niggers." At that point, it was clear that the young blacks had been caught in a racist ambush from which escape didn't seem possible.

Within moments the violence escalated. According to witnesses, one of the whites took out a gun. As he aimed it at Hawkins and pulled the trigger, he yelled, "The hell with beating them up." Four shots rang out. Tragically, two hit Yusuf Hawkins in the chest. The black teenager fell to the ground as his assailants scattered to avoid being apprehended. Elizabeth Galarza, a local resident, tried to come to Hawkins's aid as he lay on the pavement, but she was too late. She held his hand and comforted the boy as he died in what must have seemed to him like a war zone.

Yusuf Hawkins may have hoped to drive out of Bensonhurst that night in his own car, but instead he was carried out as a corpse. The hopes, dreams, and life of a sixteen-year-old honor student were extinguished by a bullet from the gun of a boy he'd never seen before.

The American dream had clouded as well for Nick Hadzinas, who had only wanted to sell his car, not ignite a violent incident that resulted in a brutal killing. After Hawkins's death, Hadzinas took the car off the market. He no longer wished to sell it. Many inquiries about the vehicle had come from individuals living in black neighborhoods. One of his friends suggested that Hadzinas wanted to be certain that no one else was hurt.

Although the young whites' brutal violence was universally condemned by city officials, it was condoned by some neighborhood residents. One young man from Bensonhurst described his feelings this way: "Look, he was black. What was he doing in a white neighborhood at nine-thirty at night?"[2]

Is this what life is like in the "land of the free and the home of the brave"? Is the American dream being destroyed by hatred and violence?

The Bensonhurst murder was spawned by racial hatred and bigotry, but the incident carries other significant implications as well. Among the most disturbing is the fact that all of the assailants were teenagers. In recent years, many towns and cities throughout America have been forced to contend with an increase in violence among juveniles. A comparison of FBI figures reveals that the number of arrests for rape committed by boys age eighteen or younger has increased. The figure rose by 14.6 percent between 1983 and 1987. Statistics on other types of juvenile crime are alarming as well. The FBI also reported that during the same four-year time span the number of arrests of juveniles under age eighteen jumped 22.2 percent, and aggravated assaults perpetrated by young people climbed 18.6 percent. It is important to note that at the time of these increases, the overall number of teenagers in the United States had declined by 2 percent.[3]

The day-to-day experiences of law-enforcement officials and social workers underscore the reality: youthful offenders throughout the nation are becoming more violent. In Denver, Colorado, two high school students stabbed a man to death. They said they committed the murder to steal the man's credit cards so they could buy camping equipment.

A fifteen-year-old girl was kidnapped from a bus station in Los Angeles, California, at knifepoint by two men. They held the young woman captive for five days and repeatedly raped her. When she finally managed to escape, she ran out to the road and flagged down the first passing car.

She pleaded with the three teenage boys inside the vehicle to help her flee. The boys told her to get into the car, but instead of taking her to a hospital or a police station, they drove to a deserted park in East Los Angeles. There she was raped again, this time by an eighteen-year-old, one of the boys who were supposedly saving her from her abductors.

In East Saint Louis, Illinois, two teenage brothers broke into a house. There they found six children, ranging in age from four to fourteen, at home alone. The elder of the intruders insisted that one of the girls, a twelve-year-old, engage in sexual intercourse with him. When she refused, he immediately slit her throat. Then the two brothers decided to kill the other children so that no witnesses would survive to identify them.

The teenage intruders forced the remaining five children to lie down on their parents' bed. Then they pulled out a gun and shot one after another in rapid succession. Amazingly, all six of the boys' victims survived the brutal assault on their lives.

Both intruders were apprehended by the police. At fourteen years of age, the younger brother had already been arrested numerous times and had an extensive history of trouble with the law. He entered a guilty plea to the charge of armed violence. He was sentenced to a prison term of 120 years. The boy's older brother later admitted his guilt as well.

Often there appears to be no discernible pattern to youth violence. Sometimes angry teenagers strike out randomly at strangers. In other instances, close friends or even family members may feel the sting of their wrath. That's how it was in the Sean Sellers case.

At seventeen, Sean Sellers was the youngest of sixty-six inmates on death row at Oklahoma State Penitentiary. Looking more like a typical high school student than a convicted and condemned murderer, the sandy-haired teenager appeared perceptive and intelligent, even likable. You might have pictured him attending football games, parties, and proms. He seemed much like any teenage boy growing up anywhere in America—but in actuality, he was not. Sean Sellers was found guilty by a jury on three counts of murder. He killed a convenience store clerk. Sean also murdered his own mother and stepfather in their bed as the couple peacefully slept. To explain his actions, Sean claimed that he committed these atrocities while paying homage to Satan.

In the vast majority of cases, youthful perpetrators of violent crimes are boys. However, at times, teenage girls may be involved as well. In California, a sixteen-year-old girl, accompanied by three male companions, went on an arson spree. The group set fire to three public schools, causing over a million dollars' worth of damage to the buildings and their contents. Still another sixteen-year-old girl, from eastern Massachusetts, repeatedly stabbed her male cousin for no apparent reason. Her victim was so severely injured that he nearly died.

At age fifteen, Paula Cooper brutally murdered seventy-eight-year-old Ruth Pelke, a Bible school teacher. Paula, along with two of her young friends, went to the woman's home on the pretense of inquiring where religion classes were being held. Not suspecting their actual intentions, the Gary, Indiana, woman invited the girls to come in while she looked up the address. When she turned her back on the girls, Paula grabbed Ruth Pelke from behind and threw her on the floor. The frail woman somehow managed to stand up again, only to be hit over the head with a heavy vase thrown by Paula.

According to Paula's courtroom testimony, she then pulled out a twelve-inch knife she'd kept hidden in her jacket. As Paula testified, "I cut her on the legs and on her arms.... All of a sudden she fell down and was lying on her back. And then I remember stabbing her in the stomach. And then I stabbed her in the chest."[4]

Paula Cooper's knife thrusts were so forceful that the blade cut through her victim's body, pierced the carpet on which Mrs. Pelke lay, and splintered the hardwood floor beneath her.

Following the murder, the young girls pillaged the house. They later claimed that they were looking for jewels and money. They found only a ten-dollar bill and the keys to Ruth Pelke's Plymouth. The girls hopped in the car for a joy ride. They ended up at a local video arcade. Finding some of their friends there, the girls offered them a ride home. One friend noticed the bloody knife on the car floor and jokingly asked if they'd just murdered someone. Paula responded with laughter.

Paula Cooper was later convicted of murder. Today she is the youngest woman on death row in America.

Perhaps the most frightening aspect of today's juvenile crime is that the deviant behavior appears to be more mechanically performed and more vicious than it was in the past. Is a new breed of young perpetrator emerging— individuals who don't feel sorry or guilty, at least initially, and who can easily shrug off their victims' suffering? Psychologist Shawn Johnston described the trend this way: "Burglars used to rob a house and then run away. Now they urinate or defecate in the home or burn it up before leaving. Thieves mugged a person and ran off. Now they beat up their victims. Or rape or murder them."[5] Although adolescence has traditionally been considered a period of anger and rebellion, many of the atrocities committed by today's youthful offenders are difficult to comprehend.

Some mental health experts believe the dynamics behind such savagely brutal attacks may be extremely complex. One hotly debated theory involves the correlation between aggression and biologically determined factors. This view attributes violent behavior more to physiological factors than to environmental causes. Various experts have theorized that violent behavior may in some ways be genetically determined. Others feel that aggressiveness may be largely due to a chemical imbalance in the brain.

Testosterone, the male sex hormone, tends to rise during puberty. Some researchers feel that high testosterone levels may be partly responsible for increased aggressiveness and violence in teenagers. It's been found that some particularly aggressive athletes and prison inmates have unusually high testosterone levels.

However, it may be too simplistic to conclude that aggression is merely a factor of biological destiny. Societies have largely been able to control or channel aggressive impulses through such basic institutions as the home, the school, and religious organizations. But in recent years, these institutions have had to contend with major internal problems of their own. An overwhelming number of children now grow up in homes headed by one greatly overburdened parent. Some parents may be desperately trying to deal with their own debilitating addiction to drugs or alcohol, or both. These parents may be unable to provide their children with a sound nurturing environment.

Unfortunately, some young people have been subjected to parental abuse and neglect for much or all of their lives. Dorothy Otnow Lewis, professor of psychiatry at New York University, has said, "Kids are being raised by more and more disturbed parents. And what this lack of parenting breeds is misshapen personalities."[6]

Without knowing why, these young individuals may act as brutally as they were treated. Because they are enraged over their parents' abuse of them, they may lash out at innocent victims. JoAnne Page, executive director of the Fortune Society, an organization that helps ex-offenders reenter mainstream society, said in August 1989, in an interview with the author, "It's rare for us to see someone who wasn't savagely abused as a child. Intense brutality marks people; it affects the way they see the world. To them the world is an unpredictable place, a jungle, and they are victims. People who feel victimized sometimes do things that damage other people, but they don't believe that different options exist for them. They feel trapped in a place where that's just the way things are."

However, not all youthful offenders come from abusive environments. It is also important to note that violent behavior among young people transcends both racial and class lines. A recent study of criminal activity among teenagers revealed that well-off communities are frequently among those affected by the rising trend in violence.[7]

This may be due to the fact that a life of ease and privilege can have negative side effects. At times children who are given numerous material benefits come to believe that they are entitled to whatever they wish. Some feel that society's rules don't apply to them because their parents will always bail them out of trouble.

Overly indulgent parents often make excuses for inexcusable behavior or try to buy their children's way out of a difficult situation by paying for whatever damage the son or daughter caused. As a result, these young people don't learn to curb their conduct. In many affluent homes where problems have arisen, the children have been given every new toy and luxury. However, one element is often missing in these homes: parental attention and supervision.

In an interview with the author in August 1989, Sergeant Nick Irons, head of the Community Services Bureau for the upper-middle-class community of Sparta, New Jersey, echoed this idea: "Unfortunately, today we look at kids as excess baggage. Presently most families are two-income households. Both the father and the mother actively pursue their own careers. The result is that in many cases kids are left to raise kids. Very often there's little supervision or real direction offered in these households. The important influences in a young person's life come from other kids. To worsen matters, easy accessibility of dangerous substances such as drugs and alcohol may intensify an already potentially high-risk situation."

Perhaps Randa Dembroff, an official of the Los Angeles County Bar Association, best summed up the problem when she said, "A workaholic parent is just as abusive as someone who physically abuses his children."[8]

Experts cannot agree on any one single cause of this disturbing increase in teenage violence. Each time a new case makes headlines, a broad range of explanations, from physiological to psychological, is offered. Since every case has its own special circumstances, generalizations do not always apply. Each young violent offender has a unique set of genes and family experiences that may have helped to mold the way in which he or she responds to stress, boredom, or depression within the social environment.

Yet regardless of the causes, the effects of increased violence among young people have been detrimental to society. In October 1989 two New York City Jewish teenagers were nearly beaten to death by a gang of fifteen to twenty young whites. The muggers had indentified the boys as Jews because they'd had on yarmulkes (a cap worn by religious boys and men). Previously, Jewish students had been warned by school officials against wearing yarmulkes after dark. The educators feared some neighborhood youths might viciously assault the students if they knew they were Jews.

The message was clear—in order to escape the violence, these young people would have to hide who they really were. It is difficult for many people to come to terms with living in this type of society. As the mother of one of the young victims stated—"This was just a ruthless attack.

Parents shouldn't have to worry that their kids can't walk the streets just because they show their beliefs."[9]

NOTES
Chapter 1

[1]*The New York Times*, 3 September 1989, p. B4.

[2]Hawkins incident quotes: *Newsweek*, 4 September 1989, p. 25.

[3]Crime statistics: *Time*, 5 June 1989, p. 60.

[4]*Woman's Day*, 30 May 1989, p. 123.

[5-8]*Time*, 12 June 1989, pp. 52-57.

[9]*New York Daily News*, 9 October 1989, p. 16.

CHAPTER

2

Teen
Group Violence

It happened in New York City's Central Park on a warm April night in 1989. A band of young black and Hispanic teenagers had gotten together and gone out seeking excitement or, as they put it, "looking for something to do." Maybe they wanted to feel powerful, to prove their strength or mastery over another person. Perhaps they were bored or angry or both.

In any case, the boys splintered into small groups of ten or less. They then began to roam the northern reaches of the park. They were searching for victims. One of the groups spied a female jogger just past a grove of sycamore trees. Police reports indicate that they chased the woman into a gully. Then the real nightmare began. For nearly half an hour, the boys beat her with a metal pipe and repeatedly slammed a fair-sized rock into her head. The youths took turns fondling the woman's body and raping her. When they'd finished, they left the woman for dead.

The jogger wasn't found for nearly four hours. At that point she was in a coma and had lost almost three-quarters of the blood from her body. Police later said that only the woman's superior physical condition had kept her alive. The jogger had suffered multiple skull fractures, and after being taken to a hospital she remained in a coma for many days. There were indications of serious brain damage.

The boys' victim was an attractive twenty-eight-year-old investment banker who had earned degrees from Wellesley and Yale. She was a young woman with a bright future, someone who had everything to live for until the night a group of teenage boys met in the park looking for something to do.

News of the incident, quickly picked up by the media, spread throughout the country. The full scope of the horror was difficult to comprehend. A new word was introduced into the nation's vocabulary—a word that would become synonymous with violence and mayhem. It was the term the boys used to describe the mischief they'd intended to do when they met that night. They'd called it "wilding."

A hard core of about seven boys were suspected and apprehended in the rape and beating of the female jogger. Following the arrests, police described the boys as haughty and smug. None expressed any guilt or remorse. While attempting to pinpoint a motive, police detectives reported that one of the boys said they did it because "It was fun. It was something to do."[1] Eventually, six of the boys were indicted for assault and rape.

A number of wilding incidents were reported at that time in New York City. Some teenagers with time on their hands and little with which to occupy themselves had unfortunately been drawn to the excitement and violence they perceived in wilding. The female jogger wasn't the only victim that night. Other groups of teens attacked a home-less man and a male jogger in the same park.

In the Bronx, the northernmost borough of New York City, a band of about thirty youths cut school to rampage through a golf course. Scattering throughout the area, they robbed and pushed bystanders. At times they forcibly took the golf clubs out of players' hands and swung them at their victims.

In many ways these wilding incidents were similar to the "wolf pack" crimes that had already raised the fears of residents in some urban areas. "Wolf pack" was a term given to a new breed of young assailants who stalk a city's streets in groups. Often they stroll the avenues in search of a "poppy love"—a well-dressed middle-aged or elderly man who was likely to be carrying cash. An especially good find would have both jewelry and "pocket prints"—the outline of a billfold within his pocket.

Wolf pack crime tends to be more methodical and organized than the seemingly random violence often associated with wilding. Young men who rob in packs often consider themselves professional thieves. Many take pride in their athletic prowess and physical stamina. Mark, a teenager who occasionally runs with a wolf pack, can do 150 push-ups in a row and claims, "I hit pretty hard for my size." Mark spoke with pride when he described Drac, another member of his group, whose training regime did not permit him to touch cigarettes or alcohol. Of his friend and cohort, Mark said admiringly, "Do you know how fast Drac can run?"[2]

Wolf packs tend to choose their victims carefully. As these young men often consider themselves accomplished thieves, they are more interested in obtaining significant amounts of cash than in violence for the sheer experience of brutalizing others. Nevertheless, their tactics often prove to be quite violent.

For example, one evening a mob of about thirty-five teens attacked an elderly man who was on his way to see a play. The boys moved in on the man from all sides. They kicked and punched him till he fell to the ground. The victim never got a good look at his assailants' faces. All he remembered was a swarm of grabbing hands and hard-hitting fists. While he was on the ground, the boys also kicked him from side to side. In a matter of moments, the incident was over. The man's assailants swiftly fled with his money and jewelry.

A similar gang raided a subway train one Sunday morning. They rampaged through car after car, assaulting victims and taking their valuables with speed and precision. Over one hundred young men divided into small bands rampaged through a March of Dimes walkathon. They robbed and beat the startled victims, then left the scene as quickly as they'd arrived.

Recent statistics indicate that violence among youthful offenders is on the rise. Although specific numbers on teen group crimes are not available, many law-enforcement officials believe that this horrifying phenomemon appears to be increasing as well. Why is this happening?

At times these attacks and robberies may be rooted in racism. Some of the attacks have been by black teens striking out at white victims. Groups of whites have also terrorized and killed black youths merely because they were in the wrong place at the wrong time. As racial tensions in crowded and often impoverished urban areas increase, it becomes increasingly difficult to dismiss these vicious gang attacks as isolated incidents.

Certainly there were strong racial overtones associated

with the wilding incident involving the Central Park jogger. A number of black leaders argued that the white-dominated media coverage of the story was tinged with a heavy anti-black bias. Black journalists as well as other spokespersons from the black community publicly criticized the mainstream media's full disclosure of the names of the juvenile suspects involved, while the identity of the young white rape victim was carefully guarded. As Father Lawrence Lucus, the black pastor of Resurrection Roman Catholic Church in Harlem, put it, "There is a belief in our society that African-American lives are not as valuable as those of Caucasians."[3] Racial tensions were further heightened when billionaire developer Donald Trump called for the death penalty for those involved in the near-fatal beating of the jogger.[4] Trump ran full-page ads in four newspapers stating, "I want to hate these murderers....I want them to be afraid." In an interview Mr. Trump stated, "I'm sick and tired of watching this kind of thing being perpetrated on an innocent public." But in a later statement Mr. Trump admitted that he was not seeking the death penalty for minors.[5]

However, some individuals claim that the attack on the female jogger and many other incidents of teen gang rape and violence are more deeply rooted in sexism than in racism. Viewing the incidents from a feminist perspective, they fear that the deep underlying sexism of these attacks on women may be obscured by the racist overtones of some of these cases. They feel that often the most disturbing aspect of teen gang violence is the savage and dehumanizing victimization of women.

As Joanne Jacobs, a columnist for the San Jose *Mercury News*, wrote of the attack on the Central Park jogger, "The talk about race misses the point. The critical element of this attack was that they were male. She was female. They were predators. She was Bambi."[6]

A hideous incident of teen group violence against a woman was the gang rape of a young mentally impaired girl in an affluent, largely white community in northern New Jersey. Word of the incident filtered through the halls of the local high school for months before police arrested five teenagers and charged them with attacking the seventeen-year-old girl.

The girl was invited to the home of two of the boys—twin brothers—on March 1, 1989. When she arrived, she found thirteen boys present. Five of the teenagers raped the girl. They also violated her with a broomstick and a miniature baseball bat. Instead of coming to her aid, the eight remaining young men watched the rape.

The victim had known two of her assailants since grammar school. Both the victim and her attackers were white. Three of the boys accused of the rape were stars of the high school football team. One of the onlookers was reported to be the son of a local police lieutenant.

Many incidents of teen group violence involving the brutalization of women may be deeply rooted in the largely unconscious sexism within our society. Very often gang rape participants do not construe their actions as rape. They may instead claim that their victim was a "nymphomaniac," that "she really wanted it bad," or that "she loved every minute of it and wanted more."

Some boys who would not commit a solitary rape may view gang rape as acceptable. These young males may regard gang rape as a means of proving their masculinity to their friends and themselves. In some ways a gang rape may be seen as a perverted rite of passage into manhood for the assailants, at their victim's expense.

It may not even matter to these rapists who the victim is. These young men are more interested in the camaraderie among the rapists and the feeling of oneness they derive from their common involvement in the rape. An individual who refuses to participate might be ridiculed or shunned by the group. It's likely that the others would challenge his sexuality as well.

But gang rape can be unimaginably brutal for the victim. Frequently the level of violence, hostility, and humiliation increases with each man's abuse of the victim. At times the extreme violence may even result in the woman's death. One such case occurred in Chicago when four teenage boys raped and then killed a female medical student. According to Cook County Deputy State Attorney Pat O'Brien, that case was solved as a result of good police work and the "defendants' inability to keep their mouths shut." O'Brien explained that "It was a badge. It was something they talked about as if it gave them status within that group of guys."[7]

In addition to racism and sexism, social class differences may sometimes be a factor in teen group violence. It's possible that some teen group violence may actually be an attack on the affluent, privileged, preppy-yuppy class by deprived and enraged ghetto youth. One proponent of this view is Dr. James Comer, a black psychiatrist at the Yale Child Study Center, who has said that one such episode seemed "as much an issue of the haves and have-nots, as it is of race."[8]

Although this might be true in some cases, teen group brutality does not always cut across sex or class lines. Groups of teens have destructively ganged up on victims of their own sex and from their own social class, in affluent as well as impoverished areas.

One such incident took place in Carl Junction, Missouri,

in December 1987. Three seventeen-year-old high school students brutally beat a classmate to death with baseball bats. The horrific deed began when the four boys drove out to a desolate wooded area on a cold December day. They had supposedly gone into the woods to honor the devil through the practice of Satanism. The first bloody ritual performed involved killing a cat. Then all of a sudden three of the boys turned on the fourth—a teenager named Steven Newberry. They chanted, "Sacrifice for Satan, sacrifice for Satan," repeatedly as they closed in on their victim.

Terrified at what was happening, Steven fled from his attackers. Unfortunately, he stumbled, and the others caught up to him. When he turned to his former friends and asked them why they were attacking him, one of the boys answered, "Because it's fun."[9]

One bat used in the assault broke in two; the others cracked under the frenzy of seventy blows.

Following the murder, the boys weighted Steven Newberry's body with rocks and threw it down a cistern along with the mutilated cat. They called it "the well of Hell," just as they labeled one of the baseball bats "the ultra-violence stick."

The boys involved in the incident seemed unlikely candidates for participation in a group murder. In his freshman year of high school one of the boys had been voted Knight of the Year. Another was president of his senior class at the time of the brutal and senseless slaying. All three of the boys who murdered Steven Newberry are now serving life sentences in prison without the possibility of parole.

The dynamics behind incidents of teen group violence can be extremely complex. A leader often emerges within the group. He is usually able to control and manipulate the others by playing on their need to prove themselves. The group leader displays a dual sense of mastery in such situations: he demonstrates his power over the victim as well as over the other boys as he subtly challenges them to imitate his actions.

Acting as a group may serve to validate the violence. On his own, an individual might not engage in criminal acts, but the group helps to negate his feelings of doubt. The participants often reason that this activity can't be wrong if everybody's doing it. Teenagers may be especially susceptible to a group viewpoint, since they are often extremely sensitive to peer pressure. Adolescent restlessness and the herd instinct—a kind of follow-the-leader mentality—tend to take over and bond group members.

Frank Zimring, director of the Earl Warren Legal Institute at the University of California, conducted a study of youth homicide in New York City. He believes that at times violent teen groups operate under the dynamics of "'government by dare'—you do it because you don't want to back out."[10]

However, perhaps the most significant aspect of acting within a group is that the individual participant remains somewhat anonymous. When a horrendous act is committed, each group member may reason that he's not really responsible because he was just one of many participants. In such instances the individuals use the group as a protective shield. They try to reason that it's the group—not the individuals who made up the group—that is accountable.

At times group participants are enabled to act viciously with their cohorts because individual thought and action mesh into a group mentality. Acting as little more than a cog in a wheel, the individual temporarily abandons his sense of self. His own values and ideals become subordinate to those of the group.

Group attacks often involve a sort of subdivision of labor. The violence necessary to disable the victim is broken down into smaller tasks. Each group member is given a job to do. He's supported in his actions by the others.

Destructive group dynamics of this sort may have played a role in the Central Park rape. The defendants later related that a fifteen-year-old boy first spotted the female jogger and then directed the others to "Go get her." A fourteen-year-old boy assisted in knocking the woman down. Once she'd fallen, he punched, beat, and kicked her. Following his lead, the other boys took turns assaulting their helpless victim. Different boys repeatedly hit her with a brick, a rock, and a lead pipe. This subdivision of tasks tends to allow each individual involved in the incident to view his role as relatively minor. However, the end result may be no less nightmarish.

The same subdivision of labor is quite common in wolf pack crime. One boy acts as a lookout. Another is assigned the job of grabbing the victim from behind in a chokehold. A third and fourth boy may push, kick, and beat the victim. One or two others are responsible for grabbing the money and jewelry.

It may be impossible to discern precisely how deeds and emotions intertwine in teen group violence. Perhaps several forces—racism, class resentment, sexism, and peer group pressure—destructively combine to dehumanize the assailants. It is also difficult to ascertain what each boy's personal conflicts have to do with his participation, and how the subdivision of labor during violent acts lessens each participant's feeling of responsibility.

How should society deal with teen group violence? Some

people plead for understanding and compassion for the criminals, while others demand more severe punishments. Suggested remedies include increased police protection, harsher penalties for juvenile offenders convicted of violent crimes, and more funding and remedial assistance to troubled inner-city communities.

However, New York Governor Mario Cuomo has acknowledged that there are no quick remedies or simple solutions to the problem of teenage violence. He said of the predicament, "We're naturally trying to find a pill-size answer and digest it and end the matter. I am not afraid to admit I don't have the answer. I would be wary of the person who thinks he does."[11]

NOTES
Chapter 2

[1]*Time*, 8 May 1989, p. 21.

[2]Wolf pack quotes: *New York* magazine, 3 June 1985, p. 31.

[3]*Newsweek*, 15 May 1989, p. 20.

[4]*The New York Times*, 1 May 1989, p. 20.

[5]*Newsweek*, 15 May 1989, p. 40.

[6]*Ibid.*

[7]*Time*, 12 June 1989, pp. 52-53.

[8]*Newsweek*, 15 May 1989, p. 40.

[9]*The New York Times*, 21 May 1989, p. 40.

[10]*Newsweek*, 8 May 1989, p. 65.

[11]*Newsweek*, 15 May 1989, p. 40.

3

"That's Entertainment"— Violence in Toys, the Media, and Sports

Any exploration of teenage violence must include an examination of entertainment and recreation in our society. American children are exposed to various forms of violence in the guise of play from the time they are toddlers.

In the late 1980s, five of the six best-selling children's toys were so-called action figures. Among these are such violence-prone characters as G.I. Joe, Voltron, Go-Bots, He-Man, Masters of the Universe, and Transformers. Action toys may exert a greater influence on their young owners than most parents realize. This is due to the frequent TV tie-ins. To enhance their toys' popularity and salability, manufacturers create cartoon shows starring their warrior-type characters. This way young viewers are offered readily available battle stories.

Although parents may think their child isn't playing with war toys but is simply watching television, there may not be a great deal of difference in the child's actual experience.

The amount of violence on these shows—which are viewed primarily by children under six—is astounding. A typical war cartoon show averages forty-one acts of violence each hour, with an attempted murder every two minutes.[1]

Recently more people have begun to question seriously the role these toys and the corresponding cartoon programs play in the formation of a young person's values. Some children own a number of these toys and know exactly when the plastic killers will spring to life on their TV screens. Even children who can't afford the toys watch the programs and fantasize about either owning the action figure or following in the footsteps of their miniature murdering heroes.

The product-based cartoon shows tend to feature dehumanized characters acting in a machinelike manner without thought or emotion. The Transformers and Go-Bots seen on TV are always engaged in destructive acts, yet the impact of their deeds is significantly minimized.

As victims are extinguished in a predictable and efficient manner, children aren't exposed to the human pain and suffering that actually go hand in hand with extreme brutality. Viewers are shielded from the genuine consequences. The end result of the abundant toys and cartoon shows is that millions of children across America are served a continuous diet of glorified and sanitized violence.

There's no doubt that these toys and shows have been a commercial success for their manufacturers and producers. Within a one-year period, action toys and their accessories had sales of nearly a billion dollars.[2] In fact, the National Coalition on Television Violence reports a 600 percent increase in war toy sales from 1983 to 1985.[3] The proliferation of war toys raises a question as to whether these playthings and the violent cartoons encourage aggressive tendencies in very young children. Are they detrimental to normal healthy development or are the violent feelings they evoke simply worked out in innocent play scenarios?

Some psychologists claim that children who habitually play with violent toys and regularly view the cartoon shows are "less likely to protest violence as a way to solve problems."[4] Some research has demonstrated that the overall effects of toy and television violence increase the probability that young children will resort to aggressive behavior in their daily lives. The toys and cartoons work in tandem: children employ the violent toys to reenact the violent behavior depicted by cartoon characters on their TV screens.

Unfortunately, children's exposure to television violence extends significantly beyond cartoon programming. Children of all ages watch violent TV shows on a daily basis. The Center for Research on the Influence of Television has revealed that children may see substantially more television violence than their parents do. Adult programs average five violent acts per hour, while programming for young people averages five to twenty-five.[5]

Mental health experts have argued that television violence encourages children to act aggressively, largely because violence is condoned on the shows they watch. In crime stories the police as well as the criminals resort to violence. Frequently much of the same aggressiveness may be discerned in both the sheriff and the outlaw. Violence is seen as acceptable behavior and a means of solving problems. Children frequently come to feel that the most effective way to deal with personal problems is through physical violence.

Psychologist Leonard Eron of the University of Illinois believes that there is a direct correlation between the amount of violence children see on television and the aggressive behavior they exhibit. His conclusions are the result of his extensive long-term research study involving eight hundred children from Columbia County, New York. Eron and a team of researchers charted the development of these children from the time they were eight until they turned thirty.

In drawing conclusions from this study, numerous factors were taken into consideration, including each child's IQ, cultural and economic background, and parental attitudes. The end results confirmed that the amount of violent television children watched at the age of eight proved to be the best indicator of how aggressive they would be at nineteen. The trends indicated by Eron's data even correlated with the number of criminal offenses some had been convicted of by the time they turned thirty.

Dr. Benjamin Spock, the noted pediatrician, feels that children who repeatedly view violence on television eventually become desensitized to the horror appearing on the screen. He claims that recent psychological experiments have conclusively shown that television violence tends to desensitize individuals of all ages. Desensitization is a process by which individuals who are at first horrified or disturbed by viewing violent acts gradually come to accept this behavior. After continued exposure, the initial shock value is lessened and the behavior is more easily taken for granted.

It has been calculated that by age eighteen the average American has seen more than fifty thousand murders or attempted murders on television, including cartoon shows. Dr. Spock feels that the eventual result of such extensive exposure will be a high degree of desensitization among the general viewing public.

The famous pediatrician stresses that a child brought up by loving and caring parents or caregivers will not necessarily be goaded into criminal activities as a result of on-screen violence. His point is that "everyone, tough or gentle, will be moved bit by bit in the direction of insensitivity, cynicism, and harshness."

In support of this theory, Dr. Spock relates a conversation that occurred nearly thirty years ago: a seasoned nursery school teacher told him that after the Three Stooges' television show became popular, the children in her class began bopping each other over the head for no apparent reason. She would admonish them for their behavior, explaining that hitting people was unacceptable, but the children showed no regrets. Often their retort was "Well, that's what the Three Stooges do." At that point it became clear to the teacher that very young children will as readily imitate violent behavior as socially acceptable actions. Children regard whatever adults do as permissible.

Dr. Spock believes it's unfortunate that American children are exposed to the degree of on-screen violence and brutality that commonly takes up a good portion of their TV-viewing hours. He also points to the fact that the United States has the dubious distinction of having one of the highest rates of murder, rape, wife abuse, and child abuse of any other nation in the world.[6]

Not all available data supports the contention that violence in the guise of entertainment indirectly helps to perpetuate brutality and cruelty. As might be expected, there is some disagreement on this point. Some psychologists insist that playing with violent toys and seeing brutality on TV is simply part of growing up and goes hand in hand with more positive types of behavior to produce well-rounded people who are in touch with the broad range of their feelings.[7]

However, most of the evidence leans toward the opposite viewpoint. In fact, it has been suggested that violence on television and in movies affects both children and adults more than most people would like to admit. The effect of staged violence intermingled with comedy, for instance, may seem innocuous. We may find ourselves laughing at slapstick incidents in which individuals are comically shot, slapped, or pushed off tall buildings. Yet when we stop and think about what we're really chuckling at, the humor fades. Some research strongly suggests that once our defenses are down in humorously charged entertainment situations, we become more likely to accept violence.

A number of groups and individuals concerned over the trend toward increased TV violence have lobbied for more government intervention in regulating programming. In the United States, legislative measures to curb TV violence are seriously under way. The Television Violence Act, sponsored by Senator Paul Simon of Illinois, has been proposed to help lessen the amount of brutality shown on TV. Yet, even if the bill passes both the House of Representatives and the Senate, public support may still prove crucial to its ultimate effectiveness. This is because the bill's usefulness would largely depend on the willing cooperation of the highly profit-minded television industry.

In addition, some factions feel strongly that no one has the right to dictate or censor the television programming available to them and their children. They believe it is crucial that such decisions remain in the hands of each individual, parent, or guardian.

Perhaps Barry Lynn of the American Civil Liberties Union best summed up the danger of censorship in his response to a church group that was in favor of new restrictions. He said, "If you cannot persuade persons to reject what you consider exploitative or unhealthy, do not ask the government to impose your will on those same persons."

The debate over violence in entertainment extends beyond TV viewing. Violent entertainment is also available in numerous other forms. It is marketed in highly salable packaging for nearly all age levels. For example, home video games, which are very popular with young people, are often extremely violent. One study revealed that 83 percent of the ninety-five most popular home video games feature violent themes. Of these, 58 percent are war games.[9]

Annually, Americans spend over $2 billion on video games such as Mike Tyson's Punchout, Rambo, Commando, and Aliens of the Evil Empire. One game called Rush'n Attack—a play on the words "Russian attack"—offers young players a choice of weapons with which to kill enemy soldiers to free American P.O.W.'s. The player may annihilate his on-screen opponent with a selection of knives, bazookas, or hand grenades.

One eighth-grade boy who's president of the players' club in his hometown spends hours each week in front of his television screen piloting military attack jets or fighting Ninja warriors. His aggressive role varies according to the game he selects. Describing how this favorite recreational pastime makes him feel, the boy said, "When I'm playing, I feel like it's me on the screen."[10]

The National Coalition on Television Violence warns that negative side effects may be associated with many of the video games that are extremely popular among young people. The coalition charted the effects of a video game played frequently by eight- to ten-year-olds. The game involved shooting interactive laser weapons at the "enemy" projected on the television screen. The findings revealed a dramatic rise—nearly 80 percent—in playground fighting immediately following periods in which the young people played the aggressive video game.[11]

In addition to television programs and warlike video games, home video movies have become extremely popular among young people in recent years. The significant increase in video outlets has dramatically raised the number and variety of films available to viewers. A sophisticated electronic entertainment industry continues to afford consumers the opportunity to watch what has been construed by some as a heavily merchandised though often brutal variety of rapes, murders, and muggings in the comfort of their own living rooms.

Every day children across America walk into video outlets to rent blood-and-gore movies they would be prohibited from viewing in a movie theater because they are under seventeen years of age. For example, in the film *Alien Prey*, a blood-dripping vampire dines on a female corpse after puncturing a hole in her stomach.

Another choice might be *Make Them Die Slowly*. This film boasts two dozen torture scenes, one of which shows a woman being sliced to pieces by a man. In the film *Flesh Feast*, creatures devour living humans. First they pull the skin off their victims' heads; then they munch on the remainder of the body.

Parents and other individuals who are deeply disturbed by the pervasive violence in home videos have urged restrictions to prevent video stores from renting violent videos to children. In addition, they've petitioned for a new

Motion Picture Association of America rating for violent films. This would enable them to decide which films would be inappropriate for their children to view. They are also working for regulations that would require video stores to display prominently the MPAA ratings of all of the films they rent.

However, the issue isn't as clear-cut as the groups suggest. Many video store owners firmly believe that it's the parents' responsibility and not theirs to police the viewing habits of minors. As in the proposed restrictions on television violence, once again the question of censorship arises. Does anyone have the right to tell other people which movies they may or may not see? Is it fair to stifle the creative efforts of any artist?

Nevertheless, critics of excessively violent home videos point to the increase in violent behavior in young people and wonder if the movies' ill effects on American youth may perhaps be underestimated. One advocate of new restrictions told of a mother who wasn't disturbed by the fact that her children had seen a number of brutal slasher films. She reasoned that no harm was done, since they didn't seem affected by the movies. Yet opponents of this type of entertainment argue that perhaps the most disturbing aspect of these videos is that they enable us to view the heinous brutality and torture of other human beings and not be affected by it.

Comic books represent still another form of entertainment for young people that has not been left unscathed by the trend toward blood and gore. In the past, comic book adventures were usually fairly innocuous. Writers tended to create humorous storylines out of innocent dating mishaps or to extol the valorous deeds of superheroes.

Frequently children today are offered comics that titillatingly blend sadism and sex into their storylines. For example, in an issue of the comic *Green Arrow*, a promiscuous woman is brutally crucified. Even Superman has been called upon to do battle against a new breed of villain. In one episode called "Bloodsport," a Vietnam veteran who has gone mad terrorizes the streets of Metropolis. Carrying a gun in each hand, he sets off on a random shooting spree, cutting down innocent passersby at whim.

Violence has also become commonplace in some spectator and recreational sports. This development is especially true in ice hockey, where many owners, managers, and coaches feel that violence is synonymous with toughness and bravery—not to mention profits. Eye-gouging, head-butting, hair-pulling brawls have become common and eagerly anticipated features of the game.

At a more vicious moment a player may thrust the blade of his hockey stick into his opponent's mouth and listen for the sound of loose teeth. Even such vital organs as a kidney or liver are often not spared the thrusts of a hockey stick during a game.

Owners are aware that crowds anxious to see blood and gore on the ice will pay handsomely for such spectator privileges. Classified ads in the video section of a magazine called *Hockey News* enticingly read, "Hockey's Bloodiest Fights and Knockouts" and "165 Hours of Good Quality Hockey Fights."

However, recently a Canadian judge took a firm measure in an attempt to curb hockey violence within the National Hockey League (NHL), whose games are played both in the United States and Canada. The case involved Dino Ciccarelli, a twenty-eight-year-old all-time leading scorer for the Minnesota North Stars.

The judge courageously convicted Ciccarelli of assaulting

Luke Richardson of the Toronto Maple Leafs during a hockey match. Dino Ciccarelli was sentenced to one day in jail and fined one thousand dollars. The judge's action was considered noteworthy, since the law had traditionally not intervened in instances of hockey violence. Hockey teams had never had to worry about criminal charges applying to their players.

The Toronto incident may have sparked the start of an attitude change on the part of the judicial system. In convicting the star player, the judge cited "the need to convey a message to the NHL that violence in a hockey game or under any circumstances is not acceptable in our society."[12]

Violence is inherent in other popular sports as well. Brutal initiations into the game of football are often common among young players. In a process that has sometimes been compared to army boot camp, young players begin to grow accustomed to brutalization. They learn to inflict and to endure pain, and they try to master certain intimidation tactics. One high school sophomore team member described it this way: "We were determined to punish, hurt, and defeat them, not for the sake of survival or territorial imperatives, but for the appeasement of manufactured egos. We had seen fans on TV chanting, 'Kill, Bubba, Kill!' It seemed glorious and glamorous."[13]

At times sports violence may spill over into family life. Super Bowl Sunday has become an American tradition for many football fans. Large numbers of men across the country follow the action on television. There may be drinking, betting, and a heightened sense of individual involvement with the plays and players.

However, some individuals may experience unpleasant consequences as a result of the game. Unfortunately, Super

Bowl Sunday is also among the busiest days at family crisis shelters across America. Although mental health professionals believe that the game in itself doesn't cause wife and child abuse, it may be a factor in escalating violence within already abusive families. A man's tendency toward violent outbursts and abuse in these situations may be aggravated by having drunk too many beers or by feeling depressed over a favorite team's defeat.

Research indicates that the violence inherent in the game itself may have something to do with the phenomenon. As Denver psychologist Dr. Lenore Walker explained it, "Winning football is about power, and violence against women is the ultimate form of power in this society."[11] The male viewer may identify with the violent players as he watches the game on TV. When his feelings of rage reach a heightened pitch, it may not matter to him that he's not on a football field. He may just seek any convenient target at which to direct his aggressive feelings. Often that target is his wife, son, or daughter.

Violent incidents related to sports are not confined to Super Bowl Sunday. Police departments and women's centers report an increase in arrests for domestic violence following Monday night football games. Unfortunately, for some, black eyes, bruises, and broken bones may be the result of entertainment tinged with violence.

It is difficult to assess the effects of this phenomenon on teenage boys growing up within these home environments. As young children some had been victims of the violence. As teenagers some continue to be victims while others silently view the sporting event along with their father's abuse of their mothers. Since in many instances children tend to follow the example set by the adults surrounding them, the larger implications for society are frightening.

NOTES
Chapter 3

[1]*Christianity Today*, 21 February 1986, p. 16.

[2]*Mother Jones*, April-May 1986, p. 12.

[3]*Christianity Today*, 21 February 1986, p. 16.

[4]*Mother Jones*, April-May 1986, p. 12.

[5]*Christianity Today*, 17 February 1989, p. 47.

[6]*Redbook*, November 1987, p. 26.

[7]*Health*, March 1989, p. 90.

[8]*Christianity Today*, 21 February 1986, pp. 16-17.

[9-11]*The Nation*, 19 December 1988, p. 673.

[12]*Christianity Today*, 17 February 1989, p. 47.

[13]*The Nation*, 19 December 1988, p. 673.

[14]*Mother Jones*, January 1987, p. 15.

CHAPTER

4

Drug
Gang Violence

Less than a twenty-minute drive from the well-tended lawns and picturesque mansions of Beverly Hills lies the run-down and impoverished area of South Central Los Angeles. The slums in this community have been largely taken over by teenage drug gangs. Here teens as young as fifteen cruise the streets in customized BMWs and Mercedes. Many carry Uzi submachine guns or Soviet-made AK-47 assault rifles. The cars are status symbols; the guns are tools of their trade. The gang members' daily lives are frequently marked by desperation, violence, and death. These young people are involved in the illegal drug trade.

Youth gangs have an extensive history in the Los Angeles area. In the 1950s they dealt marijuana and PCP, or angel dust, on a small scale. However, the recent availability of cocaine in the form of crack has created a multimillion-dollar industry, changing both the nature of the gangs' activities and their neighborhoods.

According to Sergeant Bob Sobel of the Los Angeles Sheriff's Department, "Los Angeles is now the clearing point, the center of a distribution network for the entire western United States. And it all goes through South Central." The number of young men involved is astounding. "Police say there are about 74 gangs affiliated with the Bloods, totaling about 5,000 members," Sobel says. "The rival Crips are even bigger—103 gangs and 10,000 members. Almost all of the gangs are involved in the crack trade." Steven Strong, the Los Angeles Police Department's detective in charge of gang intelligence, described the makeup of these gangs: "A typical gang might have 200 kids from thirteen to twenty-six years of age. Each gang moves anywhere between 25 and 40 kilos of coke per month."[1]

The competition and feuding between the gangs can be intense and explosive. Gangs are designated by their chosen colors, dress codes, and areas of operation. For example, the Crips wear blue, while Bloods have adopted the color red. Gang members may also use their own hand gestures, or signs.

When gang members pass one another on the street, it isn't always necessary for them to speak in order to identify themselves. The color and style of their clothing will clearly reveal their gang affiliation. Gang members wear loose pants, and for a time both the Bloods and the Crips wore Puma sneakers. The Bloods' Pumas were black suede with a red stripe and red shoelaces. The Crips' were blue. Lately, both gangs have been wearing a different brand.

The walking sticks that were popular ten to fifteen years ago are no longer used. However, many gang members wear an earring. Crips and Bloods can be further identified by red or blue bandannas worn around the head in "do-rag" style. Some gang members let their bandannas, or rags, hang from their pockets.[2]

Possession of a particular area of the city may be extremely important to a gang. The drug trade has given new meaning to the concept of turf. Once gang members bragged about the size of the area they controlled as an ego exercise, but now losing turf may mean relinquishing valuable drug-sales territory. Since a territorial invasion might entail a monetary loss, the graffiti used to delineate turf boundaries may actually be coded threats. The following graffiti sprayed on an L.A. wall is one such example: "Big Hawk 1987 BSVG 187ͼ." To translate, Big Hawk is a gang member's street name. BSVG stands for Blood Stone Villains Gang, a Blood set, or affiliate. The lower case c which is deliberately x'd out indicates that the writer kills Crips, and the number 187 refers to the section of the California criminal code for murder.[3]

In their day-to-day activities, all drug-related youth gangs are actually quite similar to one another. One reporter explained: "Members of both pick up their cocaine from big dealers in the neighborhoods who distribute them through legitimate businesses like car washes and car detailing shops; both run 'cook houses' that turn cocaine into crack. The Crips and the Bloods used to fight over turf *West Side Story*–style with switchblades and chains. Now they battle for market share with handguns; the big-time dealers who supply the gangs favor their Uzis and AK-47s."[4]

Gang violence accounted for nearly four hundred killings reported within L.A. County in 1987 alone.[5] The drug trade, particularly in crack and in rock cocaine, has transformed tough street gangs into complexly organized ghetto-centered drug trafficking organizations. An especially frightening aspect of the trade hinges on the fact that a number of L.A. gangs have now established direct connections to major Colombian smugglers, thereby ensuring a continuous supply of their highly salable if deadly merchandise.

Although the Los Angeles predicament is extremely serious, it cannot be viewed as an isolated situation. Youth gang drug trafficking is rapidly spreading throughout the country. Law-enforcement authorities report that "Dangerous as it is, the situation on the West Coast is just part of a much bigger problem. Big-city gangs in New York, Chicago, Miami, and Washington, D.C., are breaking into the crack business as well, and some are actually spreading drugs and violence to other cities all across the country. In Chicago, where gang membership has reached an estimated 13,000 after a lull in the 1970s, the infamous El Ruckns are under active investigation for drug trafficking. In New York...police are struggling to contain an explosion of drug-related violence that has left more than 500 persons dead in upper Manhattan alone during the past five years. A Miami-based gang called the Untouchables is pushing crack northward to Atlanta, Savannah, and other cities of the Southeast, where the groups is known and feared as the 'Miami Boys.'"[6]

Recent evidence suggests that drug-dealing youth gangs have begun to spread from urban ghetto areas into America's heartland. Law-enforcement authorities are investigating the L.A. gangs' movement to establish branch operations in various areas from Denver, Colorado, to Vancouver, British Columbia. In addition, Chicago gangs have begun to move into Milwaukee and Racine, Wisconsin, and Minneapolis, Minnesota.

The racial and ethnic makeup of the youth gangs tends to

vary. Gangs may be black, Hispanic, Asian, or a mixture of nationalities. In any case, ruthlessness and extreme violence seem to characterize the vast majority of these groups. Females as well as males may be involved in gang activity. Numerous gangs for girls have arisen in the same neighborhoods where male gangs thrive. According to a report in *Time* magazine, "In Chattanooga, it was *The Warriors*, a movie glorifying the camaraderie and violence of gangs in New York City, that served as the model and namesake for the first local gang. Fourteen others followed, including the Black Angels, a group with all-female membership. The result has been an overload of car-theft cases in juvenile court as well as murder."[7]

In South Central Los Angeles, fifteen-year-old Little Curl takes pride in being a member of the Black Girls 124th Strip Crips. She was quoted in a magazine interview: "I love when someone call me 'Cuz' [a code word for Crips]. It's like you got a new family who never let you down." To become a member of the gang two years ago, Little Curl had to prove herself by robbing a drugstore and stabbing a teenage clerk who worked there. She said, "Before, when I was twelve, I mugs a couple of old ladies, but that wasn't enough to be Crips, so I had to hit the store. We can do anything the boys do, most of the time better. I got my blade, and I got my .22 right here in my pocket."[8]

It may be argued that a new breed of violent young criminal is emerging from America's gang subculture. Often these individuals place scant value on human life. Most gang members appear quite willing to kill for the sake of profit. According to one expert, "Children of the underclass, weaned on violence and despair, have become bloodthirsty entrepreneurs. Some have made small fortunes marketing the cheap, explosive cocaine derivative—known as 'rock' in L.A.—with state-of-the-art firearms. Many more have wound up in prison or the graveyards."[9] Yet some of the violent outbursts between gang members have had nothing to do with business. At times, gang members engage in seemingly senseless and random violence. In countless instances gang members have killed others or put their own lives on the line in meaningless demonstrations of gang pride or in attempts to evoke a macho image.

For example, Robert Earl Dotson, an eighteen-year-old reputed member of a Chicago gang, received a forty-year prison sentence for shooting nineteen-year-old Frederick Poe to death. Poe, a member of a rival street gang, had "embarrassed" Dotson in a fistfight.

Twenty-one-year-old Keith Tyronne Fudge was sentenced to death in a court of law. Fudge opened fire on a group of teenage partygoers, killing five of them. This vicious shooting spree was his way of retaliating against a rival gang for having stolen his car.

James Galiplau, a veteran officer in the L.A. probation department, says, "There are a million kids out there who have no skills other than fighting. They are not afraid of the police, or jail or dying."[10]

Mental health experts generally agree that much of the gang members' restlessness and ready acceptance of a violence-filled existence is the unfortunate result of having known deprivation and desperation most of their lives.[11] In many instances, the long-term effects of ghetto life have left these young people without either hope or fear. They may be willing to take tremendous risks because they believe they have few choices. They are able to accept murder and mayhem because they've seen just how expendable life in the ghetto can be.

Poverty is often regarded as the overwhelming factor in increased violence among youth who feel trapped in the ghetto. Some ghetto residents believe that they are unable to break out of the vicious cycle of poverty. Teen unemployment is astoundingly high in poor urban neighborhoods. These same neighborhoods were forced to endure drastic cuts in welfare and social programs in the early 1980s. Young people who can't get a job or find any constructive means of bettering their lives often believe that there isn't much for them in respecting society's rules. Dr. Carl C. Bell, a black Chicago psychiatrist who was once a member of a gang, stated, "Violence is the weapon of the powerless." Reverend Harold Bailey, founder and director of Probation Challenge, a Chicago rehabilitative program for ex-convicts, described the complexities of the situation as follows: "We call these kids immoral, but they're amoral. They honestly don't know. They want to be macho and don't want to be put down. No one has told young murderers that when you get angry you should just sit down and think things out."[12]

Gang members also seem to have a perverse disregard for the safety of innocent people. An increasing number of gang homicide victims have been non-gang members. According to *California* magazine, "At a South Central high school a seventeen-year-old girl new to the school unknowingly wore blue Pumas—the color of the Crips—into a Blood-controlled area and was hung to death at lunchtime. A black woman in her twenties, unrelated to any gang, had her car break down in an unfamiliar neighborhood. When she got out to try to fix it she was shot to death because of the red bandanna she wore. Drive-by shootings occur with such regularity in L.A. they hardly rate a paragraph in the [newspaper]."[13]

One evening, David Thompson, a postal worker, and his wife Namora stopped at a gas station in the South Central L.A. area. The couple were on their way home from a church meeting. Suddenly, as if out of nowhere, three armed teenage gang members attacked the stunned husband and wife. First they took the couple's money and jewelry. Then they casually shot Mr. Thompson in the head. The gang members pulled his wife out of the car, jumped into the vehicle, and drove away.

Rollers, a clipped version of "high rollers," is a term reserved for gang members who've done well financially in the drug trade. Rollers tend to be in their teens or early twenties. Although they may be far from attaining kingpin status, they've managed to acquire sufficient material possessions to place them in an enviable position among their peers.

Often the rollers deck themselves out in gold jewelry and drive expensive, glamorous cars. Roger Hamrick, a community relations worker in Miami, describes the transformation of a gang member who moved to Daytona Beach, Florida, to sell crack: "When he left [Miami], he was on a bicycle. When he came back, he wore more gold than Mr. T and he was sitting in a white Mercedes. He…has two Mercedes and a Rolex watch." Bill Blanco, gang specialist from Miami, Florida, reinforced this observation: "Who you are is dictated by the gold chains, the Rolex, the car. And everybody's got a car phone."[14] In the drug trade, cellular phones are more than a mere decoration or status symbol. As communication between gang members is crucial to their business, these phones have evolved into an essential tool of their trade.

Beepers are comparably important to drug dealers. Even child recruits being initiated into the drug business are outfitted with them. According to one source, "In South Central the crack hustle starts young. Police report that kids as young as nine years old stand on the corners selling nickel and dime bags; they can make up to $400 dollars a day." Sergeant Wes McBride of the Los Angeles Police Department described the situation as follows: "Delivery boys carry beepers connecting them to dealers; there are so many of them that many schools in the area have banned telephone pages. The kids in class were getting beeped to go deliver dope."[15]

Those who are trying to bring young people away from gangs and back into society's mainstream face a difficult task. The promise of power, excitement, and money associated with gang membership has strong appeal to individuals who see themselves as having few alternatives. As Los Angeles police detective Kevin Rogers said of the situation, "In school, these kids are told to work real hard and study, get a job at Burger King, become a manager, and at twenty-eight they'll have a house with a mortgage—and they laugh. They'll tell you they can make more money and have better clothes than you right now standing out on the corner selling rock."[16]

Unfortunately, many young people model themselves after gang members like "Five Fingers" Charlie. They are impressed with the apparent ease with which he acquired material possessions. At fourteen Charlie owned three cars. In addition, he boasted a $300,000 annual income derived from drug sales. Charlie's day in the sun was short, however. He lost everything when he fell victim to an occupational hazard. He was arrested by police and spent over a year in a correctional institution. "Five Fingers" Charlie is now back in school as a condition of his probation. Despite his experiences, along with many others like him, he still feels the fast-money lure of the drug trade. "I want to be a lawyer," he said. "But once you have been with a gang, it's hard to get out."

Their large numbers, financial resources, and propensity toward violence have combined to make drug-dealing youth gangs a serious challenge for law-enforcement authorities. As Sergeant Bob Sobel of the Los Angeles Sheriff's Office said, "We're seeing 15- to 20-year-old millionaires from cocaine. They've got electronic police-detection systems, sophisticated weapons—better equipment than we have."[17]

Yet there are serious drawbacks to youth gang membership. A gang member's life may not always be as glossy as the shine on his new car. It's an existence filled with terror and violence, leaving scant space for any remnant of human sentiment. A gang member never knows when it's all going to end, when he's going to be arrested, maimed, or killed. Each day could be his last. As one member of the Crips put it, "Maybe someday soon I will bleed to be Crips. I ain't afraid no more. I seen a lot of Crips die and it looks easy. It don't hurt to die. It kills you tryin' to stay alive here. We all kinda expect to be killed, with all the shootin' we do. It's more of a surprise to wake up every morning."[18]

NOTES
Chapter 4

[1] Los Angeles Police Department quotes: *Newsweek*, 27 April 1987, p. 35.

[2] *California* magazine, July 1987, p. 73.

[3] Graffiti example: *Newsweek*, 28 March 1988, p. 23.

[1]*Newsweek*, 27 April 1987, p. 35.

[5]*People*, 2 May 1988, p. 42.

[6]*Newsweek*, 28 March 1988, p. 42.

[7]*Time*, 18 April 1986, p. 17.

[8]*People*, 2 May 1988, p. 45.

[9-10]*Time*, 18 April 1988, p. 32.

[11]*Newsweek*, 28 March 1988, p. 22.

[12]*Ebony*, December 1987, p. 92.

[13]*California* magazine, July 1987, p. 73.

[14]*Newsweek*, 28 March 1988, p. 24.

[15]*Newsweek*, 27 April 1987, p. 36.

[16]*California* magazine, July 1987, p. 73.

[17]*Newsweek*, 27 April 1987, p. 36.

[18]*People*, 2 May 1988, p. 45.

5

Date
or Acquaintance Rape

Estelle—that is not her real name—spoke in a barely audible whisper as she related her painful story. The high school girl said she had never been very popular with boys and as a result hadn't gone on too many dates. She was thrilled when J. asked her out on two consecutive Saturday nights. She'd known and liked him for a long while and thought that perhaps now she was finally going to have a boyfriend. The couple went to a movie, and afterward J. drove out to a deserted beach. Estelle thought the setting was wonderfully romantic. She and J. could talk, look at the stars, and listen to the surf rolling in.

Unfortunately, her date had another scenario in mind. Within moments of their arrival, J. began to roughly kiss and fondle Estelle all over. She told him to stop, but his sexual aggressiveness persisted. Estelle had wanted him to like her, but she never wanted what happened next. J.

continued to ignore Estelle's protests. He ended their evening together by raping his young date on the beach.

Estelle had been a virgin at the time of the rape. Her daydreams about J. hadn't included him forcing himself on her.[1]

Estelle was a victim of what is now commonly called date rape. Date or acquaintance rape is a rape committed by someone the victim knows. Often such rapes remain unreported because the incident is never clearly identified as a crime that is punishable by law. A rape committed by a date or acquaintance may be especially difficult to label because the rapist and the victim know each other. They may have dated, worked together, or attended the same school or place of worship.

However, date or acquaintance rape cannot be dismissed as an innocuous incident. Our society cannot afford to think that an excited young man enticed by a provocative girl on a date simply got carried away and went too far. Rape is not passionate love, seduction, or the consequence of an inexperienced young man's sexual adventures. It is brutal physical and emotional violence against a woman.

Whether the rapist points a gun at his victim's head or merely pins her down using the weight of his body, the result is the same. The aggressor forces the victim to submit to him regardless of her feelings or the consequences she'll be left to face. It is an act characterized by the rapist's domination and his victim's humiliation. The fact that her rapist's face was familiar can never make the woman any less a victim or soften the impact of the crime.

Dr. A. Nicholas Groth, a Massachusetts clinical psychologist and a leading sexual assault specialist, said, "Misconceptions abound because of the mistaken notion that rape is a violent expression of sexual desire or lust. Rape is not about sex per se. Instead, rape is the sexual expression of anger or aggression."[2]

The most recent statistics indicate that date or acquaintance rape may in fact be on the rise. Teenage girls are among those who are especially at risk. Though it can happen to women of any age, in 38 percent of reported rape cases, the victims ranged in age from fourteen to seventeen.[3] In addition, a study at a rape prevention center in Maryland revealed that 92 percent of the teenage girls interviewed indicated that they'd been sexually assaulted by someone they knew.[4]

Despite the fact that only 45 percent of the rapes reported to the police are committed by a date or an acquaintance, it is highly likely that this often unreported crime is substantially more pervasive. Professionals who counsel rape victims have claimed that the actual incidence of date rape is grossly underestimated in official statistics. Those who monitor rape crisis hotlines have revealed that at times up to 80 percent of their calls are from date or acquaintance rape victims.[5]

In instances of rape by a date or acquaintance the victim frequently blames herself for what occurred. Not realizing that what happened to her can't be considered anything less than rape, she may feel isolated and filled with doubts about her own judgment and her ability to have a healthy normal relationship. One teenage date rape victim was still trying to comprehend what happened a year later. She described her feelings this way: "I thought it was my fault. What did I do to make him think that he could do something like that? Was I wrong in kissing him? Was I wrong to go out with him?"[6]

Young girls may also too easily believe the outmoded notion that in some way their behavior specifically "led the boy on," and therefore the subsequent rape was justified. Unfortunately, this notion may be reflected in the reactions of nearly everyone who learns about the rape, from the girl's parents to the members of the jury who will hear her case if it ever reaches a courtroom.

Wearing a short skirt or a low neckline or not wearing a bra can never be considered an excuse for the brutal crime of rape. Yet, unfortunately, a survey of California high school boys showed that 54 percent thought that rape was justified if the girl was a "tease."[7]

Frequently women hesitate to report date or acquaintance rape. Too often they persist in believing the myth that if they did not physically retaliate against the attacker, then what happened cannot be considered rape. However, the reality of the situation is that a woman is raped any time she is forced to have sex against her will, regardless of whether or not she physically resists. Even if the woman agreed to go out with the man, even if she agreed to kiss or embrace him, she still retains her right to say no to anything further and to have her decision respected.

Some women may actually believe that once a man has become sexually aroused, he has to have sex in order to avoid extreme physical discomfort. This is not true. In actuality, there is no difference between a male's and a female's need to have intercourse after either has become sexually aroused. A man who is aroused still retains the ability to control himself, and it is crucial that young women be aware of this fact.

Another reason date or acquaintance rape frequently goes unreported is that women fear their complaints will not be taken seriously by the authorities. Often the woman worries that her assailant will counter her charges by claiming that she agreed to have sex and that, as a result, she will not be believed. Too often this assumption is correct. Unfortunately, a number of myths surrounding rape tend to cloud the issue further. To many people a rapist must be a stranger, someone who creeps up on a woman from behind a row of bushes or in a deserted parking lot and forces her to have sex with him at either gunpoint or knifepoint. In reality, however, there is no "typical rapist." A rapist can be someone whom his victim knew well, trusted, and even cared for.

As Florida State Attorney Jerald Bagley stated, "Despite the terrifying brutality, rape remains one of the most difficult crimes to prosecute. Many jurors hold that if a woman is not bruised, scarred, or obviously emotionally devastated, she cannot have been forced to have sex against her will. If a woman is a victim of date rape, they suspect she must have misled her attacker."[8]

It may be difficult to pinpoint the precise causes of a case of date or acquaintance rape, but it's essential to view the crime within its societal context. The environment in which a boy grows to manhood will naturally exert a strong influence in shaping his values. Children learn the importance of valuing other human beings from the adults around them. Unfortunately, many young people don't have an opportunity to see healthy loving relationships.

Arnold Goldstein, director of the Center for Research on Aggression at Syracuse University, has stressed how the lack of suitable role models may begin early on, in the home: "Ideally, kids learn about sexuality by watching loving parents. Unfortunately, all too often, rather than kissing the wife, the husband yells at her."[9]

Many young boys grow up in homes in which their mothers or sisters are physically or sexually abused. Yet, even boys from loving homes, boys who have taken sex education courses at school, come of age in a society that glorifies machismo. They listen to rock music with lyrics that condone violence and brutality against women. These recordings are packaged in album covers that suggest acceptance of female bondage or subjugation. They watch home videos in which women are simultaneously raped and tortured. Sex and violence become intimately intertwined, and some young boys pick up the notion that it's acceptable to victimize women.

When interviewed by the author in August 1989, Nora Ramos, general counsel for Women Against Pornography, stated, "There's a ten billion dollar pornography business in this country. It's a major industry that socializes men to believe that women are appropriate targets for violence. As a result, it's not surprising to hear men who've committed sex crimes say that they found it thrilling to hurt a woman. Young boys, beginning to form their sexuality, are at a particularly vulnerable stage."

It is important to remember that no one is born a rapist. Sexual violence is the consequence of social conditioning: it is not biologically determined behavior. As anthropologist Peggy Reeves Sanday of the University of Pennsylvania stated, "Men who are conditioned to respect life…do not violate women."[10]

In date or acquaintance rape, a young woman's traditional social conditioning may tend to heighten an already potentially explosive situation. Often teenage date or acquaintance rape victims report that they found it difficult to be forceful in fending off the nice boy who one night turned into their assailant. Many young girls still grow up thinking that it's not seemly to be forceful or assertive in their relationships with boys.

One high school girl said of an acquaintance who raped her, "I never considered punching him or doing something really drastic. I guess I was a 'nice girl' and you didn't do that even if somebody was being un-nice to you."[11] Another girl described her reaction this way: "It didn't occur to me that it was okay to hurt him, to kick him...or punch him in the eye. Good girls don't do that. You sort of just lie back and let this happen and then you deal with the consequences."[12]

One psychologist and date rape expert from Auburn University related how a young victim quietly protested as she was being raped in a man's room at a college fraternity house. When asked why she didn't scream out during the attack, she admitted that she didn't want to embarrass the boy in front of his fraternity brothers.[13]

Often the victims of date or acquaintance rape are told that they should have been more alert to cues from the man that there might be difficulties ahead. The woman may be told that if she hadn't gone out with or trusted that seemingly nice guy, if she hadn't allowed herself to be alone with him, or if she hadn't been drinking, the rape wouldn't have taken place. Some victims later report that although they suspected that something wasn't right, they didn't flee from the situation because they didn't want to seem rude or immature. Nevertheless, lack of experience in interpersonal relationships or even exercising poor judgment doesn't mean that a woman deserves to be raped.

Date rape victims often find themselves in a situation where they are forced to survive not only the assault but also a popular culture that promotes violence against women and an unsympathetic societal view of their plight. Sometimes a date rape victim's initial reaction may be that she'll never feel clean and whole again. Emma, who was raped at seventeen, described her feelings as follows: "I locked the door and cried. Then I went into the bathroom and I took a bath and I took a shower and another bath and another shower. It wasn't until I was drying myself off that I caught a look at myself in the mirror and realized that my whole upper body, my neck, my chest, was covered with marks— hickeys. I was repulsed. I was so disgusted. I felt dirty and violated. I didn't want to leave the bathroom, so I just sat on the floor with my towel around me, crying."[14]

After a date or acquaintance rape, the teenage victim may need the help and support of her family and friends more than at any other time in her life. Yet too often, because of the nature of the crime committed against her, these avenues of comfort may be closed to her. Among the most common reactions to the victim's plight are blame and disbelief. Some girls find even close friends doubt their story, and they give up on telling anyone else.

In other instances, the date rape victim's friends take the matter lightly. The victim may be told that it's "no big deal" or that she is taking herself too seriously. One victim who was a virgin until she was raped was congratulated on finally having grown up. The girl's friend never saw her personal devastation, anger, and humiliation.

Barriers may also be present between date or acquaintance rape victims and their families. Topics such as sex, choice of dating partners, and curfews can be highly emotionally charged issues. This may be especially true in instances in which the rapist proves to be someone whom the victim's parents did not approve of.

One date rape victim who turned to her mother for support related her parent's reaction as follows: "The first thing I can remember her saying was, 'Well, Holly, I don't know what you expected.' And that just crushed me. I wanted someone to say, 'We still love you, it's okay.'"

Some teenage girls become so anxious at the prospect of their family's reaction that they remain silent. They'll try to deal with the aftershock of date rape by themselves rather than risk diminishing their family's perhaps idealized view of them. A high school date rape victim remarked, "I felt I couldn't go to my parents, because the fact that I had had sex with David [a former boyfriend] would arise, and somehow my loss of virginity would be worse than the rape in their eyes."[15]

Tragically, for many teenage girls, the date rape may be the first or nearly the first time they have sexual intercourse. That's what happened to Lynn, a high school junior, who allowed her boyfriend to accompany her to her baby-sitting job. After the children were asleep, he raped her as they were watching television together. Fifteen-year-old Jenny, also a virgin, was raped by a college boy who drove her home from a party.

Since so many young date or acquaintance rape victims were virgins prior to the incident, their feelings about sex, love, and relationships in general may become grossly distorted if they do not receive counseling or have an opportunity to work out their feelings. Yet many teens hesitate to tell anyone what happened. As a result, these girls may feel isolated and abandoned. They are forced to rely solely on their own inner resources to sort out their feelings and begin the healing process. To worsen matters, the young man remains anonymous and free to choose still another victim.

Since date or acquaintance rape doesn't usually entail brutal beatings or the use of weapons, we might hope that the trauma would be less than that for women raped by strangers. However, in actuality, the reverse may be true. Researchers Bonnie L. Katz and Martha R. Burt of the Urban Institute in Washington, D.C., found that date and acquaintance rape victims "rate themselves less recovered than do stranger-rape victims for up to three years following their rape experiences."[16] Andrea Parrot, a date rape expert from Cornell University in Ithaca, New York, feels that these results may have much to do with the fact that "since an acquaintance-rape victim often represses recognition of her experience, she may carry the effects of the assault for a longer time than a stranger-rape victim who may seek counseling or other support more quickly."[17]

Date or acquaintance rape cannot be pushed aside and forgotten. In some instances, the effects may be devastating. Sherry—that is not her real name—a fifteen-year-old who excelled in athletics, lived with her family in a northern state near the Canadian border. Sherry swam, rode horses, and was an exceptional skier. However, in her town, hockey was the favorite sport. Therefore, Sherry was especially excited when her friend's family invited her to accompany them for a weekend trip to a teen hockey tournament in a nearby town.

Several of the boys playing on one of the teams had grown up and attended school with Sherry and her friend. During the tournament weekend a few of those boys broke into the motel room Sherry and her girlfriend shared. Two fifteen-year-old boys along with a fourteen-year-old grabbed Sherry, removed some of her clothes, and fondled her body. They left the room, only to return moments later, saying that they wanted to apologize. Instead, one of the boys again assaulted Sherry in the same manner as before.

At first, Sherry and her girlfriend decided against telling anyone about what had occurred. However, Sherry changed her mind when she returned to school and learned that two of the boys had been bragging about having had sex with her. Sherry's parents decided to pursue the available legal options and subsequently pressed charges against the boys. Sherry's assailants were suspended from the hockey team for one game.

At that point Sherry and her family became the target of a good deal of community pressure to drop the charges. Friends, neighbors, and even strangers called Sherry's home. Adult supporters of the youth hockey association were among the most strident in their opinion that Sherry had overreacted to the incident. They were anxious to dismiss the matter as little more than a boyish prank. Their uppermost concern was that the boys be allowed to continue to play hockey without any outside interference or distractions.

Attending school soon became intolerable for Sherry. Some days she faced harassment; other times everyone would agree to ignore her. Frequently her classmates shouted obscenities at her when she passed them in the halls or on the street.

Four days after the initial court hearing of her case, Sherry took an overdose of aspirin. She recovered after a two-week stay in the hospital. The following fall Sherry and her three assailants entered the same high school. Several weeks after the term started, two of the boys pleaded guilty to the charge of sexual assault. The third boy was found guilty at a later date.

All three have been placed on probation until they turn nineteen years of age. In addition, the judge ordered them to do community service work and to pay all of Sherry's medical bills.

The case was over, but Sherry's ordeal continued. Two of the boys who attacked her had turned into "overnight stars" of the high school's hockey team. The boys were admired by much of the student body, and as a consequence of their extreme popularity, Sherry continued to be harassed.

Now many of Sherry's former friends no longer wished to associate with her. Once she found a threatening note in her locker saying that she ought to be killed for taking those boys to court. Sherry was forced to face a painful irony every day of her life. Her attackers were regarded as heroes, while she as a victim became an outcast.

Sherry's life seemed filled humiliation and she saw no available means of escape. That June she locked herself in the family car, which was parked in the garage. Sherry rolled up the windows and let the engine run. She was later found dead of carbon monoxide poisoning. On the car seat next to her lay a teddy bear, some tissues, and a photograph of her family.[18]

Fortunately, not all teen date or acquaintance rape cases end so tragically, but there is nevertheless cause for concern. It is imperative that date or acquaintance rape victims be taken seriously and be offered the help and support necessary for recovery.

A number of innovative programs have been developed to combat the rising tide of date and acquaintance rape. Some colleges have revised their student conduct codes specifically to prohibit rape, and they have established immediate hearing procedures for incidents occurring on campus. In addition, on some campuses new living arrangements may be made immediately if the victim and the accused rapist reside in the same dormitory complex. A number of colleges have appointed special task forces to monitor sexual assault cases on the premises and to distribute information on how to avoid being raped.

In some high schools, information and skill-sharpening techniques to defend against date or acquaintance rape have been incorporated into the sex education and health curriculums. Additionally, numerous secondary schools have developed lists of referral counseling services for rape victims.

At times it may be impossible to avoid date or acquaintance rape. In those instances it's crucial that the victim not blame herself for what occurred. She must always try to remember that date or acquaintance rape is not just morally wrong for young men. It is also a crime and must never be reduced to anything less.

NOTES
Chapter 5

[1]*Parents*, April 1989, p. 198.

[2]*Ebony*, October 1988, p. 108.

[3]*Redbook*, July 1988, p. 4.

[4]*Teen*, March 1986, p. 10.

[5]*Redbook*, July 1988, p. 4.

[6]Robin Warshaw, *I Never Called it Rape: The MS. Report on Recognizing, Fighting, and Surviving Date and Acquaintance Rape* (New York: Harper & Row, 1988), p. 15.

[7]Warshaw, p. 43.

[8-9]*Ebony*, October 1988, p. 108.

[10]*Journal of Social Issues*, Fall 1981, p. 6.

[11-13]Warshaw, p. 53.

[14]Warshaw, p. 21.

[15]Warshaw, pp. 78–79.

[16]Warshaw, p. 125.

[17]Andrea Parrot, "Strategies Parents May Employ to Help Their Children Avoid Involvement in Acquaintance-Rape Situations," paper presented at the New York State Federation of Professional Health Educators Convention, November 1983, Binghamton, New York.

[18]Warshaw, pp. 121-23.

CHAPTER

6

School
Violence

Seventeen-year-old Chester Jackson was a football star at his Detroit high school. However, one day he was seen running through the halls rather than across the football field. Jackson was running for his life. Moments later he was fatally shot by a fourteen-year-old freshman. The two boys had quarreled during lunch period. Their argument ended with Chester Jackson's death.

In recent years, numerous schools have become increasingly violent. Far from being places for learning, many schools are now dangerous areas. Instead of carrying pencils and notebooks, some students come to school armed with knives and pistols. In some schools it's not uncommon for violent incidents to occur in the hallways, cafeteria, rest rooms, and even in the classrooms.

Depending on the area, some schools may seem more like battlefields than educational institutions. For example, in New York City, an eighteen-year-old arrived at the side entrance of a junior high school armed with a fully loaded Uzi. The young man had loaded his weapon with hollow-point bullets, which explode on impact. Fortunately, police arrived and the youth was arrested before anyone was harmed. Frequently, however, school personnel as well as students have been victims of violence. In St. Petersburg, Florida, a high school student started a commotion in the school cafeteria when he brandished a handgun. Two assistant principals and a teacher were shot before the weapon could be taken from the student.

In certain instances, the situation has reached crisis proportions. For example, in an elementary school boys' room in the Bronx, a borough of New York City, one teacher received more than twelve stab wounds. When another instructor questioned an older teenager who entered an elementary school playground, the boy suddenly turned on the teacher. Wielding a baseball bat with both hands, he brutally assaulted the teacher in the head and upper body. The teacher nearly died as a result of the attack.

Teachers have been kicked and punched and have had rocks and other objects thrown at them for merely trying to maintain order in their classrooms. One teacher was brutally beaten by a student merely because he asked the boy to put out his cigarette while in class.

Violent incidents and unchecked aggression appear to be more widespread in overcrowded inner-city schools, but to some degree schools throughout the country have become less safe in recent years. In a nationwide Gallup Poll taken in the late 1980s, 3 to 4 percent of the teenagers surveyed said they had been physically attacked at school.[1]

One victim of intimidation and violence was a fifteen-year-old high school freshman named Bob who lived in a rural area of Oregon. As he was somewhat shorter and more slightly built than the other boys, he quickly became a target for ridicule and harassment. Three bullies at school joined together to taunt their classmate at nearly every opportunity. Bob was pushed, kicked, and knocked off his bike. At times, the boys even threatened to kill him. Their continued harassment took its toll on the young victim. Bob had difficulty eating and often awoke during the night after having terrifying nightmares. He also had trouble concentrating in school, and before long, his grades began to drop.

Every time Bob went to school it was like stepping into a boxing ring. He always had to be prepared for an attack. Leaving school did little to alleviate the terror, since the boys seemed to enjoy ganging up on Bob during the bus ride home. Bob's mother visited the school to report what was happening to her son. But the faculty didn't take her complaints seriously.

Bob's school was not located in a crime-riddled urban neighborhood. He resided in a sparsely populated quiet rural district, hardly the type of place where anyone would suspect that verbal abuse would erupt into assault. Yet that's exactly what occurred.

One day the bullies managed to box Bob into a corner during a crowded assembly program. The three then took turns hitting him in the head as they used their bodies to conceal their victim from passersby. As a result of the head injuries he sustained, Bob later suffered from severe headaches, dizziness, and occasional seizures. The full extent of his injuries has not yet been medically determined.

Bob eventually transferred to another school. Although this time his adjustment went smoothly, it was difficult for the teenager to forget his earlier experience. Bob's mother filed legal suits against the boys who attacked her son, their parents, and the school administration. She stated that the outcome of the suits was not as important as letting her son know that there were alternatives available to him and people he could turn to for help.

The school bully has had a long history in American folklore. Small children chant the nursery rhyme about Georgie Porgie who harassed his female classmates until they cried. Today some parents may tend to view a bullying child almost with a sense of pride. To them he may appear to be a young person who's not afraid to stand up for himself, someone who won't allow others to push him around. However, in actuality, school bullies may be children with serious behavior problems.

According to David G. Perry, Ph.D., professor of psychology at Florida Atlantic University, "Bullying is not a normal part of childhood behavior." Studies have shown that individuals who are overly aggressive as young children are far more likely to be involved in criminal activity as adults. Their victims generally do not fare very well either. Children who are continually taunted and harassed by bullies often become insecure and experience a great deal of anxiety.

Dan Olweus, a Norwegian psychologist, conducted a good deal of research on schoolyard violence. His findings indicate that bullies, or overtly aggressive young people, are usually insensitive to their victims, have average self-esteem, and take a fairly positive view of their violent behavior.[2]

However, causes other than bullying have combined to contribute significantly to increased school violence. One reason frequently cited for these problems is that in recent years the responsibility for disciplining children has shifted from the home to the school. This coincides with reports from a number of first grade teachers who say that frequently young students enter their classrooms without seeming to know that hitting other children is not acceptable behavior.

Another reason for the rise in school violence is that increasing numbers of teens are using alcohol and drugs. Substance abuse among young people has unfortunately become commonplace. These substances cloud judgment and lower inhibitions so that some disputes result in violence.

In recent years, schools have also had to contend with students who appear to have less regard for order and regulations than did former generations. One California-based poll compared discipline problems in the 1940s with those faced by educators today. In the 1940s the major problems perceived by school administrators included chewing gum, getting out of place in line, making noise, and not putting paper in wastebaskets. In the late 1980s, the major concerns cited were drug abuse, rape, robbery, assault, arson, and bombings.³

The range of criminal activity that may take place in any school spans a broad base. Reports of incidents include theft of lunch money and jewelry as well as rape and even murder. The smaller offenses, such as petty theft, bullying, and threats of bodily harm, which usually accompany extortion demands, are too frequently part of everyday school life for many children. Often these incidents are not taken seriously by school administrators. Those involved may merely be reprimanded or mildly disciplined.

In any case, frequently the harassment of other students continues. In fact, a nationwide study conducted by school principals revealed "that the greatest concerns expressed by seventh and eighth graders were theft, bullying, and vandalism perpetrated by their peers."[1]

Many young people have no choice but to attend school even though they feel intimidated by some of their classmates. They simply do their best to adjust to a difficult situation and hope that somehow they'll get by. One sixteen-year-old New Jersey boy expressed his feelings about the predicament as follows: "You get used to it and learn not to leave anything valuable around. I never wear my good watch on gym days."[5]

Even students who haven't been victimized by criminal activity in school are still adversely affected by its existence. In some situations, these children may be forced to pursue their education in an atmosphere of fear. Crime, or even the fear of being physically affected by it, can disrupt any learning situation.

Unfortunately, in some schools a pervasive unwritten code of silence protects those individuals who commit crimes. Often intimidated by the threat of bodily harm, victims hesitate to report crimes either to their parents or to school authorities. Even teachers who have been robbed or assaulted by aggressive students have been discouraged by their superiors from notifying the police. At times, a principal may imply that a competent teacher would be able to handle the matter alone and wouldn't wish to jeopardize the school's reputation by going to the authorities.

Principals are often extremely anxious to keep their schools' problems from being publicly exposed. Wishing to avoid criticism from parents, school boards, and the community at large, some principals have made light of violent incidents in the hope of preserving their image as able administrators.

In addition to threats and violent attacks against students and faculty, some schools have had to contend with extensive vandalism. According to national PTA statistics—reported in *Woman's Day* (11 February 1986)—over $600 million of vandalism is done in schools throughout America each year. This exceeds the amount of money spent annually for textbooks! All students lose when tax dollars that might have been spent on new innovative programs or equipment are instead allotted to repair damage or replace items as a result of vandalism.

At times the amount of damage done by individual students seems astounding. For example, two New Jersey boys vandalized their school system's buses. The monetary damage amounted to over $60,000, and the school had to be closed for two days due to the lack of transportation. A student from a middle-class section of Portland, Oregon, was so disappointed in his semester grades that he hurled a packet of explosives into the school office. He destroyed his records along with those of the other students, and he caused $43,000 worth of damage to the building.

The reality of violence on school premises has forced administrators to resort to more stringent security measures than ever before. Some city and school authorities now require that students wear ID badges, and many classrooms are equipped with silent alarm systems.

Numerous schools regularly conduct random locker searches, and in varoius areas, undercover police have been brought in to protect both students and faculty. In Los Angeles, California, undercover police protection has been essential in order for some schools to function. The Los Angeles United School District's police absorb approximately $13 million of the schools' $3.3 billion budget.

Three hundred police officers patrol the school buildings and premises. About 150 work in plainclothes; the remainder wear police uniforms and ride in marked cars. All of the officers are armed and are empowered to book suspects at local police precincts.

Other efforts to combat the problem of violence on school property have included the use of metal detectors. These devices have been installed at the entrances to some schools in order to let students in while keeping firearms out. Although metal detectors may not be viewed as a pleasant addition to school equipment, some administrators feel they're necessary to provide security for their students. For example, metal detectors have been used successfully on a random basis in Detroit, Michigan. Before their installation, fifteen students were expelled for carrying guns.

Some schools have experienced a great deal of trouble maintaining safe school premises. Lindbergh Junior High School in Long Beach, California, underwent frequent dangerous disruptions when physical education classes were conducted outdoors. This was largely due to the fact that the school was adjacent to a housing project. At times, project residents threw bottles and rocks at the children playing in the schoolyard. Once an arrow was shot into the yard, and on at least two occasions guns were fired at the students. A student playing basketball in the yard was wounded by a sniper's bullet. A gym teacher conducting her class outdoors was nearly hit as well.

Initially, community leaders tried to intervene to stop the violence. When the incidents persisted, school officials decided to erect a permanent barrier to separate the school from the surrounding area. As a result, workmen built a concrete wall 10 feet high and 900 feet long to protect the children from the housing project attackers.

In various places across the nation, efforts are under way to combat school violence. At times dynamic and dedicated principals have set a new tone in extremely violent schools. Some have accomplished this by ridding the school of hard-core problem students and by instituting and enforcing strict rules and disciplinary procedures. Many students who are anxious to get a good education and attend school in a safe environment are grateful for the changes.

Often these principals attribute their success to a good staff, a great deal of energy, and community support and involvement. They establish high standards for their students and do their best to enable young people to meet their expectations. For example, in Chicago, Illinois, principal Marva Collins turned around a public school, renamed Westside Preparatory School, bringing national acclaim to a once dangerous and disorderly school environment. Her personal brand of discipline forbids gum chewing and gang jewelry. When a defiant youth struts into the building, Ms. Collins might react as follows: "I put my arm on their shoulder and say, 'Darling, is your hip broken?' or 'You're going to have to take out that earring.'"

In addition to hiring outstanding principals with ambitious plans for their students, some schools have begun disarmament programs. Previously, Boston students carrying knives, guns, and other weapons to school were expelled. Now they may have an opportunity to attend the Barron Assessment and Counseling Center, a program designed to encourage youths to exchange their weapons for books.

At the center, students spend five and a half hours a day

on schoolwork. The remainder of their time is devoted to learning how to deal with their anger in a nonviolent manner. This alternative school is also known for its frightening field trips. For instance, students visit Boston's Charles Street jail to speak to inmates and learn what prison life is really like. Franklin Tuker, director of the center, says, "It's a way of letting the kids know that the customary smack on the hand is going to stop."[6]

The smattering of successful innovations may inspire others. Throughout America's history, schools have largely held their own as educational mainstays. According to the old song, school was the place where the three R's—reading, 'riting, and 'rithmetic—were taught. Let us hope it will never become an institution dominated by robbery, rape, and rival gangs.

NOTES
Chapter 6

[1]*NEA Today*, February 1988, p. 13.
[2]*Parents*, April 1988, p. 195.
[3]*Time*, 1 February 1988, p. 54.
[4]*Jet*, 4 July 1988, p. 14.
[5]*Woman's Day*, 11 February 1986, p. 50.
[6]*Time*, 1 February 1988, p. 56.

CHAPTER

Juvenile
Justice

The problem of youthful offenders and juvenile justice is actually international. Estimates indicate that at least 83 nations are grappling with serious levels of crimes committed by minors.

In the Soviet Union, teachers are trained to spot signs of troublesome behavior among their students. Under the Soviet system, however, delinquent children are not held solely accountable for their own actions. Special officers from the Soviet militia may be assigned to monitor their parents' behavior. If the parents are determined to be problems as well, the state may require that they attend special seminars to improve their parenting skills and subsequently their children's behavior.

Children who experience adjustment difficulties both in and out of school may be targeted as high-risk youths by Soviet militia officials. Their records may be sent to a bureau established to oversee the welfare of minors. Depending on the circumstances, the bureau may require these children to attend special after-school recreational programs. Some of the children in these programs are required to meet periodically with an adult who tracks their school performance as well as their overall behavior. Teenagers between fourteen and seventeen who actually commit crimes in the Soviet Union are likely to find themselves in court. A two-person team comprising a teacher and a social worker will assist the judge in determining an appropriate penalty.

Teenagers who commit serious offenses may be sent to a juvenile labor colony. The majority of young people sent to these detention centers remain there from six months to one year. Inmates at the labor colony are expected to continue their studies at their grade level. In addition, they are required to learn a trade to work at after completing their lessons. Inmates are not permitted to see their friends from home. Their families are allowed to visit them only once every three months, and packages from home may be received only every two months.

Other countries have tried to handle the problem of juvenile crime in different ways. In recent years, Great Britain has seen a sharp rise in crimes committed by youthful offenders. Police records indicate that as of 1985 approximately half of all known criminals there ranged in age between fifteen and nineteen. It's also been reported that nearly a quarter of the teenage males have been convicted of at least one crime.

There has been a significant public outcry against the rising crime rate in Great Britain. As a result, the judicial system has adopted a somewhat tougher attitude in handling youthful offenders. This "back to justice" trend has resulted in stiffer sentences for youths. The courts have also taken over forms of discipline that were once the responsibility of the schools.

It is especially interesting to note that within recent years juvenile crime in Sweden has skyrocketed. One survey revealed that well over half of the violent crimes in Sweden are committed by teenage boys. Sweden is an affluent democratic country with a high overall standard of living. Therefore, poverty, unemployment, and poor housing cannot be blamed for the youth crime wave.

Some feel the problem of teenage crime may be related to affluence and an overabundance of leisure time. They feel that perhaps young people with access to cars, cash, and drugs may be more likely to get into trouble than individuals with fewer resources available to them.

In addition, general life-style changes throughout Sweden may have contributed to the nation's present delinquency problem. At one time Sweden was largely an agricultural nation. Children worked on the farm under the close watch of their parents and grandparents. Now that the nation has become increasingly modern and industrialized, children often receive less supervision than in the past.

The court system in Sweden tends to be somewhat permissive. Punishment for offenders generally takes the form of fines, probation, and suspended sentences. A high rate of recidivism (committing further crimes) has caused Swedish authorities to consider revamping their present juvenile justice system. Currently over 60 percent of the youths between eleven and thirteen who have been convicted of one crime are arrested for another offense within five years.[1]

A comparison of international juvenile crime patterns yields some revealing statistics. For example, the country

with the highest level of juvenile crime (criminal acts committed by individuals between fifteen and seventeen years of age) is Japan. Australia has the second highest rate.[2]
It's obvious that the Unites States has a serious problem with juvenile offenders. America has a long history of trying to deal effectively with the predicament. During colonial times (the 1600s) punishment for young people tended to be swift and harsh. As a rule, juvenile offenders did not receive more lenient treatment than adults accused of comparable offenses. For example, in the Massachusetts colony, a teenager over sixteen years of age who had cursed at or hit his parents could receive the death penalty.

As time passed, however, attitudes toward juvenile offenders softened. In New York, a movement for juvenile-justice reform sprang up in 1825. It was argued that young people forced to serve out harsh sentences with hardened adult criminals would too easily be led into a life of crime themselves.

In an attempt to remedy matters, the New York Society for the Reformation of Juvenile Delinquents opened America's first reform school. The institution's goal was to turn around the lives of young offenders through a regimen of prayer, hard work, and schooling. It's ironic that although the founders of the reformatory stressed the importance of kindness in dealing with wayward youths, the school dealt very severely with those who did not adhere strictly to its rules. Youths who broke those rules were whipped and beaten, shackled with leg irons, or left for extended periods in solitary confinement.

By 1855 various reform measures for juvenile delinquents were being tried across the nation. The New York Children's Aid Society removed troubled children from crime-ridden urban environments and placed them with farming families in rural parts of the country. The Massachusetts State Reform School for girls initiated small group residences where a few girls lived together under the direction of a counselor.

In those early days a young person didn't have to commit a crime to land in a reform school or group home. Children were sent there for being idle or keeping company with wayward youths. Parents could place their children in a reformatory without even providing a reason for doing so.

Later, in the 1880s, new waves of immigrants came to the United States. Young immigrants faced poverty, language barriers, and discrimination as they tried to adjust to a new culture.

As a result, an overwhelming number of young people who ended up in court were immigrant children. Law-enforcement authorities and judges soon realized that often these children stole because their families were hungry. It was determined that these children would benefit more from rehabilitative assistance than from severe punishment. In response to this need, our present juvenile justice system was born.

Supposedly, the new juvenile justice system would take over where parents had failed, or in areas in which special assistance was necessary. In juvenile court, young people didn't have to go through a jury trial; instead, they appeared before a judge. Youths who passed through the juvenile justice system weren't shipped off to prison. They were sent to training schools, where it was hoped they'd be set on the proper path to a crime-free life.

In the late 1960s, however, the juvenile justice system came under severe public scrutiny. A presidential commission assigned to study its strengths and weaknesses concluded that the system had failed to achieve its goals. The major criticism was that these courts tended to concentrate on petty offenses while youths guilty of extremely serious crimes were for the most part permitted to go free. At juvenile court, serious offenders continued to be treated like children—gently scolded and shown how to improve.

As Massachusetts Senator Edward Kennedy said of the system at the time, "If juveniles want to get locked up, they should skip school, run away from home, or be deemed a problem. If they want to avoid jail they are better off committing a robbery or burglary."[3]

By the close of the 1970s, the juvenile justice system had begun to be more stringent in dealing with youthful offenders. However, there is no national juvenile justice system in the United States. Therefore the legal procedures aren't uniform throughout the country and methods of dealing with youthful offenders differ sharply from state to state. Despite changes in some areas, many critics feel that the juvenile justice system is still largely ineffective. They believe that this is because the juvenile justice system continues to function under the basic assumption that its purpose is to guide rather than to punish youthful offenders.

For example, offenders who appear in juvenile court do not receive a criminal record. Therefore, even if they've been in trouble a number of times, a new judge will have no way of knowing their history. The idea is to protect youthful offenders from stigma and prejudice, but at times the results may be disastrous for their victims.

In addition, many juvenile cases never even reach the courts. Police sometimes let youthful offenders off with a warning. Other cases are dismissed by prosecutors who feel that the crimes don't warrant a judge's time and attention. It has been estimated that nearly 14 percent of the crimes committed by juveniles never even reach juvenile court.[1]

Opinions as to how juvenile offenders should be dealt with span a broad spectrum of philosophies. Many victims have cried out against the leniency that presently typifies the juvenile justice system. These individuals believe that young people capable of acting as savagely as any brutal adult do not merit the tender treatment traditionally reserved for minors. Yet other factions feel a more humane answer lies in early intervention. It's difficult, however, to see how early intervention could have averted the tragedy involving Arthur Bates.

Even before Arthur was four years old his mother had noticed that her son was a troubled child. She had asked a caseworker for help with him. By the time Arthur turned ten, there were signs that he had been abused, but authorities were unable to ascertain by whom. He was taken by the state, and he spent time in a series of detention centers and residential mental health facilities.

However, no one seemed able to make any progress with the troubled youth. Physicians at a Houston hospital determined that the young boy needed help, but they said he was ineligible for their program because he wasn't "out of touch with reality," a criterion for admission to their facility. Bates was subsequently admitted to a mental health facility in Waco, Texas. After a few months, doctors there declared that they couldn't help him, and they discharged Bates. Finally, the state sent Arthur Bates to a privately run psychiatric facility. He remained there for a full two years at a cost of $113,000 per year, but the hospital's professional staff wasn't able to make any progress with the boy either.

Finally, a judge returned Arthur Bates to his home. Bates's social worker had described the situation as tragic. Everyone involved with the case was aware that Arthur wasn't well. Yet their resources had run dry. At that point, it was nearly impossible to find a facility capable of accepting a young person with Arthur's mental and emotional problems.

The Texas Youth Commission's chief counselor Matthew Ferrara described Bates as a "multihandicap kid"—a young person with a combination of legal, emotional, and behavioral problems. Ferrara added, "Multihandicap spells trouble. It also means no treatment." This may be at least partly due to the fact that neither the mental health centers nor the holding centers are equipped to deal with young people like Bates.

Once released, Arthur Bates was continually in trouble. He appeared in juvenile court a number of times on charges of auto theft, trespassing, and burglary. Since Texas law prohibits treating juveniles as adults before they are fifteen years of age, Arthur retained his status as a juvenile offender. As a result, he only spent seven months in reform school.

In fact, Arthur had been home for about three months when he raped and murdered Lillian Piper. Arthur claims that he didn't actually set out to kill anyone that day. He was merely looking for a house to break into and rob. However, Ms. Piper, who ran a popular day care center in town, had the misfortune of being home when the young teenager randomly targeted her house.

Bates didn't leave the house immediately after he raped and murdered Lillian Piper. First he helped himself to a dish of butter pecan ice cream from the freezer. Then he drove off in the dead woman's Cadillac. He was stopped by the police about an hour later. Bates confessed to the crime immediately, but he was also quick to inform the police that he would be shielded from the law's retaliation. The boy calmly told them, "You can't do anything to me. I just fourteen."[5]

NOTES

Chapter 7

[1]All figures pertaining to worldwide crime are from *Scholastic Update*, 3 November 1986, pp. 26-27.

[2]Statistics provided by the International Criminal Police Organization (Interpol), St. Cloud, France.

[3]*Scholastic Update*, 3 November 1986, p. 3.

[4]*Ibid.*

[5]*Newsweek*, 24 November 1986, p. 94.

CHAPTER

8

Crime
and Punishment

In response to the extreme and senseless brutality demonstrated by some youthful offenders, various jurisdictions altered their approach to juvenile crime. The majority of states now permit juveniles to be tried as adults if they are over a certain age and are charged with heinous murders. Recently these provisions have been extended to cover less serious crimes such as manslaughter and armed robbery.

However, this approach hasn't been as successful as its proponents had hoped. Their goal was to remove violent young people from society's mainstream where they might harm others. But problems with incarceration exist as well. Unfortunately, the funding necessary to build adequate facilities in which to retain convicted young people has lagged far behind the public rhetoric of politicans.

As a result, youthful offenders may end up in adult facilities, which are often little more than schools for crime. One survey revealed that 6,300 juveniles out of approximately 49,000 in custody across the country had spent time in adult prisons.[1] In many ways, this desperate measure denies young prisoners both adequate protection and an opportunity for constructive reform.

Overcrowding in our prison system has reached epidemic proportions. The prison population has more than doubled since 1980.[2] New prisoners are continually sent to federal and state correctional facilities that are already teeming with inmates. In addition to those already convicted, thousands more await trial in local jails throughout America. Sometimes they remain there for months, waiting for an available court date. In some facilities, the conditions are deplorable. At times there aren't any beds left, so prisoners are forced to sleep on floors and in hallways.

In some instances prisons have become so overcrowded that authorities have been forced to release inmates before they have served out their sentences in order to make room for new arrivals. For example, Los Angeles County has available jail space for approximately 13,000 inmates. However, at one point over 22,000 prisoners were dangerously crowded into the existing lockups. To make room for the newly sentenced, over 10,000 inmates were released prior to the completion of their sentences.

In Oregon prisons there is room for approximately 3,000 inmates. Over 5,000 inmates have been crowded into those facilities. Authorities have been forced to release one inmate for every new one taken in.

Studies on overcrowding in prisons indicate that most "life" sentences end before the convict has spent ten years behind bars. Some people feel that in such instances the system does little more than recycle violence back onto the streets.

So far, forty-two states have been put under court order to reduce overcrowding in their prisons. This forces correctional officials to play a risky game of releasing inmates whom they perceive to be less dangerous to make room in the prisons for muggers, rapists, and other violent criminals. At times, these officials make errors in judgment. One Georgia prison discharged a youth who was awaiting trial on car theft and drug charges. Within an hour of his release, he was picked up by police for trying to rob a man on an Atlanta street.

The unfortunate reality is that despite the fact that prisons are filled beyond their capacity, there has been no reduction in crime. In the early 1980s there was a slight decline in the number of serious crimes committed by youths, but now the tide has turned in the opposite direction.

Some claim that the rising crime rate is related to the vast influx of drugs into America, but it is unwise to dismiss other causes as well. Unfortunately, many youthful offenders have a revolving-door relationship with prison cells. Over two-thirds of those convicted return to the lockups.[3]

In view of the overcrowding, the lack of funding for new facilities, and the high rate of recidivism, those who work with youthful offenders have tried hard to find alternatives to traditional prisons and detention centers. To that end, a number of new programs have been explored. Earn It, founded by Judge Albert T. Kramer of Quincy, Massachusetts in 1975, is the country's largest juvenile restitution program. In this program local businesses provide jobs through which offenders earn money to pay their victims' medical expenses and damages. Over sixty-five state and local restitution programs have been based on this model.

The program has also been adopted in Germany, where it is known as *Das Earn It*.

In an interview with the author, Paul R. Schneider, Ph.D., project director of RESTA (Restitution, Education, Specialized Training and Technical Assistance), a program operating under the auspices of the Office of Juvenile Justice and Delinquency Prevention in Washington, D.C., expressed his feelings about why he regards restitution as an appropriate sentence for juvenile offenders. He stressed that through restitution, the young person learns accountability and becomes familiar with the damage that can result from his actions. An explicit contract is drawn up between the offender and the victim. The youth is asked to establish a payment schedule. Dr. Schneider explained that if the young person isn't working, most restitution programs will help him get a job, and as a result he may also come away with some useful skills.

According to Dr. Schneider, many of these young people have had a troubled past. There have been problems at home, at school, or in another setting. A restitution program can be helpful because all of a sudden the youth isn't in the troubled situation any longer. He is now working, earning money, and making good on a promise. Paul Schneider added that this may be the first time in their lives some of these youths have been successful at something.

Another unusual rehabilitation program for youthful offenders is the Florida Environmental Institute, or the Last Chance Ranch. The ranch is a privately run detention center that houses approximately twenty-five of the state's most violent juvenile offenders.

The program at the Last Chance Ranch is strict as well as extremely physically challenging. New arrivals are immersed in the "work ethic" for their first two years at the site.

They are assigned such tasks as digging ditches, doing construction work on ranch facilities, and performing ranch maintenance chores. The ranch is located in remote Glades County, Florida, and is surrounded by alligator-filled swamps on all sides. As a result, few inmates try to run away.

After a period of training and good behavior, inmates are moved from tents to air-conditioned barracks. In the later phases of the program, they are gradually prepared to return home. Once home, they are placed in jobs while remaining in contact with a counselor. If someone on probation gets into trouble, he is returned to the facility. Half of the ranch graduates stay out of trouble. This is an excellent record, considering the type of violent offender the facility handles.

Still another program especially designed with juvenile offenders in mind is the Center for Research on Aggression, at the University of Syracuse, New York. There juvenile delinquents learn ways to inhibit their aggressive behavior. Through a program called "skills streaming," which has been adopted by correction facilities in a number of states, young offenders learn new ways to cope with real-life situations.

The program's routine of training in fifty day-to-day coping skills includes learning how to handle fear of failure, how to follow directions, and how to face pressure. Young offenders also learn how to deal with their anger con-structively and how to make moral decisions.

Another innovative alternative for juvenile offenders is Chicago's Intensive Probation Service (IPS) program. The three-tiered program was designed as an alternative to placing hard-core juvenile offenders in overcrowded deten-tion facilities. During the program's first phase, offenders spend a month in detention in their own home. They are not permitted to leave their residence. During the second phase, they can leave the house only to attend school and counseling sessions. Some are permitted to hold down a job. Participants in the program aren't allowed to have friends visit them at their homes. These strict guidelines are enforced through visits by a probation officer five times a week. Gradually, privileges may be restored and offenders may be permitted to go out in the evening and to see friends. In time, the probation officer's visits will decrease to three times a week and later perhaps once a week. Although the IPS program is tough, it tends to be effective. More than three out of four long-term teen offenders have stayed out of trouble after participating in IPS.

A fairly new method known as "shock incarceration" is becoming an increasingly popular prison alternative for young offenders between seventeen and twenty-five years of age. Under shock incarceration, portions of state prison facilities are sectioned off into areas modeled after army boot camps. Inmates in these programs usually rise at dawn, dress and eat in silence and may only speak when addressed by someone in authority.

The rules are strict, the work menial and exhausting, and the discipline severe. An inmate who deviates from the routine in any manner my be required to immediately drop to the ground to do fifty push-ups. Throughout the program, inmates are subjected to verbal degradation and abuse. The hope behind the program is that the rough treatment will help the inmates to turn their lives around.

Does the boot camp approach to prison work? Proponents of these programs claim that they take youthful offenders off the streets and offer them a realistic taste of what life in prison would be like. Critics of the program point to the fact that boot camp "graduates" return to prison at about the same rate as those released from traditional programs. Boot camp critics also stress the unlikelihood of changing deviant behavior patterns through insults and excessive exercise.

Another recent trend in juvenile law enforcement involves holding parents responsible for their children's crimes. For example, in California, parents can be fined or jailed for allowing their children to become gang members. Florida parents may now face jail terms if their child injures another minor with a gun owned by the parent. A number of states impose fines on parents if their children are consistently truant from school. Currently, twenty-nine states and the District of Columbia have won a federal waiver to evict families from public housing if one of their children is caught using or selling drugs.

There is evidence that many recently enacted laws regarding parental responsibility were born out of the frustration and futility experienced by schools and law-enforcement agencies in attempting to subdue out-of-control teens. The idea behind these laws is to force parents to be responsible for their children's behavior. There is some controversy over both the effectiveness and the legality of such statutes, however.

One embarrassing case occurred in Los Angeles when the district attorney's office tested the new law by charging a mother with failing in her duties as a parent because her son had been active in a street gang. The D.A. didn't know that prior to being charged this woman had enrolled in a parenting course to improve her skills in raising her children. Realizing that they wouldn't be able to convince a jury that this mother hadn't tried to be a more effective parent, the prosecutors dropped the highly publicized case.

There are other problems associated with the new laws as well. Some individuals feel that the new parental liability laws smack of Big Brotherism because they allow the state to intrude in the child-rearing process. Another problem is that these new laws may discriminate against poor parents. Under a 1988 Wisconsin law a woman lost her welfare benefits when her fifteen-year-old daughter continued to be truant from school. As a result, the entire family became homeless.

Sadly, the end result of these new statutes may be that both parents and youthful offenders receive a mixed message from law-enforcement bodies. For instance, the Supreme Court ruled that sixteen-year-olds convicted of murder may be treated as adults and sentenced to death. But if sixteen-year-olds are treated as adults in such instances, how can parents be held responsible for the behavior of children that age?

Perhaps much of the confusion stems from the fact that an increasing number of judges now admit that they can no longer handle the increasingly violent crimes committed by out-of-control juveniles. As a result, courts and legislatures have imposed greater responsibility on the parents to control these troublesome children. However, the frightening truth is that no one is sure how to control teen violence on a broad scale.

Since teen violence transcends social, economic, geographical, and racial boundaries, it is difficult to come up with solutions that will apply to every case. Nevertheless, maintaining a grip on the situation has become a primary concern of many educators, legislators, parents, and law-enforcement officials across the country. Unfortunately, as we continue to search for answers, juvenile crime is rapidly becoming an intrinsic though ugly aspect of our society.

NOTES
Chapter 8

[1]*Newsweek,* 24 November 1986, p. 94.
[2]*U.S. News & World Report,* 31 July 1989, p. 17.
[3]*Time,* 29 May 1989, p. 28.

Further Reading

Books

Berger, Gilda. *Drug Abuse: The Impact on Our Society*. New York: Franklin Watts, 1988.

Booher, Dianna D. *Rape: What Would You Do If...?* Englewood Cliffs, N.J.: Julian Messner, 1981.

Campbell, Anne. *Girl Delinquents*. New York: St. Martin's Press, 1981.

Kleiman, Dean. *A Deadly Silence: The Ordeal of Cheryl Pierson, A Case of Incest and Murder*. New York: Atlantic Monthly Press, 1988.

Landau, Elaine. *On the Streets: The Lives of Adolescent Prostitutes*. Englewood Cliffs, N.J.: Julian Messner, 1987.

Lee, Essie. *Breaking the Connection: Getting Off Drugs*. Englewood Cliffs, N.J.: Julian Messner, 1988.

Weiss, Anne E. *Prisons: A System in Trouble*. Hillside, N.J.: Enslow Publishers, 1988.

Articles

Came, Barry, and Dan Burke, "Gang Terror," *McLean's*, 22 May 1989.

"L.A. Lawless," *Economist*, 2 July 1988 (gang warfare in Los Angeles).

"School for Hard Knocks," *Time*, 13 June 1988 (New York City schools crack down on violence).

Sullivan, Robert, "A Lesson Not Learned," *Sports Illustrated*, 7 April 1986 (British soccer fans still violent).

Tooley, Jo Ann, "Lessons in Violence," *U.S. News & World Report*, 13 February 1989.

List of Organizations

The following are organizations working to prevent violence:

Batterers Anonymous
1269 N.E. Street
San Bernardino, CA. 92405

Center To Prevent Handgun Violence
1400 K Street N.W. Suite 500
Washington, D.C. 20005

EMERGE: A Man's Counseling Service on Domestic
Violence
280 Green Street
Cambridge, MA. 02139

Institute Against Violence
1199 National Press Bldg.
Washington, D.C. 20045

International Coalition Against Violent Entertainment
P.O. Box 2157
Champaign, IL. 61820

National Coalition Against Domestic Violence
1000 16th Street N.W. Suite 303
Washington, D.C. 20036

National Coalition on Television Violence
P.O. Box 2157
Champaign, IL. 61820

Stop War Toys Campaign
Box 1093
Norwich, CT. 06360

Task Force on Families In Crisis (Domestic Violence)
4004 Hillsborough Road Suite 223B
Nashville, TN. 37215

Index

Abuse. *See* Children, abuse of

Acquaintance rape, 61-73

Adult influence. *See* Parents

AK-47 assault rifles, 49, 51

Alcohol, 20, 45-46, 79

Alien Prey, 42

Aliens of the Evil Empire, 41

American Civil Liberties Union, 40

American dream, 11-13

Angel dust, 49

Arson, 16

Asian teenagers, 52

Australia, 88

Automobiles. *See* Cars

Bagley, Jerald, 65

Bailey, Harold, 55

Barron Assessment and Counseling Center, 83

Bates, Arthur, 91

Bell, Carl C., 55

Bensonhurst (Brooklyn, N.Y.), 11-13

Bigotry, 13

Biological factors, 17, 66. *See also* Parents

Black Angels, 53

Black Girls 124th Strip Crips, 53

Black teenagers, 12, 23, 27, 52

Blanco, Bill, 56

Bloods (gang), 50-51

Bronx (N.Y.), 25

Bullies, 78-80

Burglary, 17

Burt, Martha R., 69

Campus rape, 72

Carl Junction (Missouri), 29-30

About the author

Elaine Landau received her B.A. degree from New York University and her master's degree in library and information science from Pratt Institute.

She has worked as a newspaper reporter, an editor, and a youth services librarian, but believes that many of her most fascinating and rewarding hours have been spent researching and writing books and articles on contemporary issues for young people.